POST-TRUTH

The MIT Press Essential Knowledge Series

POST-TRUTH

LEE MCINTYRE

The MIT Press | Cambridge, Massachusetts | London, England

This book was set in Chaparral Pro by Toppan Best-set Premedia Limited. Printed and bound in the United States of America.

Library of Congress Cataloging-in-Publication Data

Names: McIntyre, Lee C., author.
Title: Post-truth / Lee C. McIntyre.
Description: Cambridge, MA : MIT Press, 2018. | Series: The MIT Press essential knowledge series | Includes bibliographical references and index.
Identifiers: LCCN 2017034497 | ISBN 9780262535045 (pbk. : alk. paper)
Subjects: LCSH: Truth. | Truthfulness and falsehood.
Classification: LCC BD171 .M39 2018 | DDC 121–dc23 LC record available at https://lccn.loc.gov/2017034497

10 9 8 7

For Andy and Jon
Fellow lovers of wisdom

The very concept of objective truth is fading out of the world. Lies will pass into history.

—George Orwell

CONTENTS

SERIES FOREWORD

The MIT Press Essential Knowledge series offers accessible, concise, beautifully produced pocket-size books on topics of current interest. Written by leading thinkers, the books in this series deliver expert overviews of subjects that range from the cultural and the historical to the scientific and the technical.

In today's era of instant information gratification, we have ready access to opinions, rationalizations, and superficial descriptions. Much harder to come by is the foundational knowledge that informs a principled understanding of the world. Essential Knowledge books fill that need. Synthesizing specialized subject matter for nonspecialists and engaging critical topics through fundamentals, each of these compact volumes offers readers a point of access to complex ideas.

Bruce Tidor
Professor of Biological Engineering and Computer Science
Massachusetts Institute of Technology

As I write this—in the spring of 2017—there is no hotter topic of conversation than post-truth. We see it in the headlines and on TV. We overhear it in conversations at restaurants and on the elevator. This presents both an advantage and a challenge, for how to write about something that is still so new, evolving, and controversial?

This book will likely be different in tone from others in the Essential Knowledge series, for its topic is unique. The notion of post-truth was born from a sense of regret by those who worry that truth is being eclipsed. If not overtly partisan, this at least presumes a point of view: that facts and truth are endangered in today's political arena.

Given this context, in the chapters that follow it would be impossible to achieve the kind of dispassionate neutrality that one might expect in an academic book. Indeed, to do so would be to engage in a kind of false equivalence that is the hallmark of post-truth itself. The "other side" of the post-truth debate does not consist of people who defend it—or think that post-truth is a good thing—but those who deny that a problem even exists. Yet (unless my aim is that of a debunker) to presume to write a book about post-truth is to admit that there is a problem. In my analysis I will therefore strive to be honest, but I cannot promise to be balanced. When the mistakes fall disproportionately on one side, it is no respect for the notion of truth to pretend that everything is even.

Some may wonder whether the idea of post-truth is really all that new. Isn't it just synonymous with propaganda? Aren't "alternative facts" just falsehoods? But it is not that simple. While there is some historical precedent for our current situation—which we will examine—it would be wrong to try to reduce post-truth to something else. To say that facts are less important than feelings in shaping our beliefs about empirical matters seems new, at least in American politics. In the past we have faced serious challenges—even to the notion of truth itself—but never before have such challenges been so openly embraced as a strategy for the political subordination of reality. Thus what is striking about the idea of post-truth is not just that truth is being challenged, *but that it is being challenged as a mechanism for asserting political dominance.* And that is why one cannot shy away from politics if we are going to understand what one must "essentially know" about the idea of post-truth.

ACKNOWLEDGMENTS

I would like to thank several people for their contributions to this book. First and foremost, my wife Josephine has always stood by me and supported my ideas, wanting nothing more than to see me do work that I believe in. Her advice has been crucial in helping me to make this a better book. I am lucky to have a daughter and son, both of whom share my love for philosophy, who also read this manuscript with a critical eye. I am grateful to Louisa and James for helping me to make numerous improvements to both style and substance.

Special thanks go out to my friends Andy Norman and Jon Haber, who offered numerous comments—and criticisms—that helped me to shape this project. It goes without saying that neither of them is responsible for the final content, but their inspiration as honest lovers of argument and ideas has been so great that I would like to dedicate the book to them. Julia Robinson was an incisive commentator on the manuscript and Diana Rodriguez was an excellent debating partner when I was first considering the ideas that are expressed here. Bryan Barash helped me with a perfectly timed conversation about fake news. I thank them all.

I am fortunate to have had three excellent reviewers, all anonymous so I cannot thank them here by name, each of whom made important critical comments and helped me to improve my final draft.

Finally, I owe a great debt of gratitude to my editor Phil Laughlin; without his vision and guidance, this project never would have happened. I am also grateful to all of the other expert staff at the MIT Press, who make me proud whenever I publish with them. From editing to design and marketing to publicity, they are always a pleasure to work with, especially on what is now my third book with them. Here Judith Feldmann, my copy editor, deserves special thanks for saving me from a number of infelicities in a project that had such a short timeline.

I understand that this book will delight some and enrage others. For this and any remaining mistakes, I am solely responsible.

WHAT IS POST-TRUTH?

In times of universal deceit, telling the truth will be a
revolutionary act.

—George Orwell

The phenomenon of "post-truth" rocketed to public attention in November 2016, when the Oxford Dictionaries named it 2016's word of the year. After seeing a 2,000
percent spike in usage over 2015, the choice seemed obvious. Among the other contenders on the shortlist were
"alt-right" and "Brexiteer," highlighting the political context of the year's selection. As a catch-all phrase, "post-
truth" seemed to capture the times. Given the obfuscation
of facts, abandonment of evidential standards in reasoning, and outright lying that marked 2016's Brexit vote and
the US presidential election, many were aghast. If Donald
Trump could claim—without evidence—that if he lost the

election it would be because it was rigged against him, did facts and truth even matter anymore?[1]

After the election, things only got worse. Trump claimed—again with no facts to back him up—that he had actually won the popular vote (which Hillary Clinton had taken by nearly 3 million votes), if one deducted the millions of people who had voted illegally. And he doubled down on his claim that—despite the consensus of seventeen American intelligence agencies—the Russians had not hacked the American election.[2] One of his handlers seemed to embrace the chaos by arguing that "there's no such thing, unfortunately, anymore as facts."[3]

After being sworn in as president on January 20, 2017, Trump offered a string of fresh falsehoods: that he had the biggest electoral victory since Reagan (he didn't); that the crowd at his inauguration was the largest in US history (photographic evidence belies this and Washington, DC, Metro records show subway ridership down that day); that his speech at the CIA resulted in a standing ovation (he never asked the officers to sit). In early February, Trump claimed that the US murder rate was at a forty-seven-year high (when in fact the Uniform Crime Report from the FBI showed it to be at a near-historic low).[4] The latter seems particularly egregious because it picks up on an earlier fib that Trump had told at the Republican convention, while searching for a way to push the idea that crime was on the rise. When challenged on this, Newt Gingrich (who was a surrogate for Trump at the time) had the following incredible on-camera exchange with CNN reporter Alisyn Camerota:

> **CAMEROTA** Violent crime is down. The economy is ticking up.
>
> **GINGRICH** It is not down in the biggest cities.
>
> **CAMEROTA** Violent crime, murder rate is down. It is down.
>
> **GINGRICH** Then how come it's up in Chicago and up in Baltimore and up in Washington?
>
> **CAMEROTA** There are pockets where certainly we are not tackling murder.
>
> **GINGRICH** Your national capital, your third biggest city—
>
> **CAMEROTA** But violent crime across the country is down.
>
> **GINGRICH** The average American, I will bet you this morning, does not think crime is down, does not think we are safer.
>
> **CAMEROTA** But it is. We are safer and it is down.
>
> **GINGRICH** No, that's just your view.

CAMEROTA It's a fact. These are the national FBI facts.

GINGRICH But what I said is also a fact. ... The current view is that liberals have a whole set of statistics that theoretically may be right, but it's not where human beings are.

CAMEROTA But what you're saying is, but hold on Mr. Speaker because you're saying liberals use these numbers, they use this sort of magic math. These are the FBI statistics. They're not a liberal organization. They're a crime-fighting organization.

GINGRICH No, but what I said is equally true. People feel more threatened.

CAMEROTA Feel it, yes. They feel it, but the facts don't support it.

GINGRICH As a political candidate, I'll go with how people feel and let you go with the theoreticians.[5]

One might imagine a no less chilling exchange in the basement of the Ministry of Love in the pages of George Orwell's dystopian novel *1984*. Indeed, some now worry that we are well on our way to fulfilling that dark vision, where truth is the first casualty in the establishment of the authoritarian state.

The Oxford Dictionaries define "post-truth" as "relating to or denoting circumstances in which objective facts are less influential in shaping public opinion than appeals to emotion and personal belief." In this, they underline that the prefix "post" is meant to indicate not so much the idea that we are "past" truth in a temporal sense (as in "postwar") but in the sense that truth has been eclipsed— that it is irrelevant. These are fighting words to many philosophers, but it is worth noting that this is much more than an academic dispute. In 2005, Stephen Colbert coined the term "truthiness" (defined as being persuaded by whether something *feels* true, even if it is not necessarily backed up by the facts) in response to George W. Bush's excesses in relying on his "gut" for big decisions—such as the nomination of Harriet Miers for the US Supreme Court or going to war in Iraq without adequate proof of weapons of mass destruction. When the term was coined, "truthiness" was treated as a big joke, but people aren't laughing anymore.[6]

With the largely fact-free campaign over Brexit in Great Britain—where hundreds of buses advertised the bogus statistic that the UK was sending 350 million euros a week to the EU[7]—and the growing use of disinformation campaigns by politicians against their own people in Hungary, Russia, and Turkey, many see post-truth as part of a growing international trend where some feel emboldened to try to bend reality to fit their opinions, rather than the other way around. This is not necessarily a campaign to say that facts do not matter, but instead a conviction that facts can always be shaded, selected, and presented within a political context that favors one interpretation of truth over another. Perhaps this is what Trump's chief surrogate, Kellyanne Conway, meant when she said that press secretary Sean Spicer had intended to present "alternative facts" regarding the size of the crowd at the inauguration,[8] when Trump seemed miffed by official US Park Service photos showing thousands of empty seats.

So is post-truth just about lying, then? Is it mere political spin? Not precisely. As presented in current debate, the word "post-truth" is irreducibly normative. It is an expression of concern by those who care about the concept of truth and feel that it is under attack. But what about those who feel that they are merely trying to tell the "other side of the story" on controversial topics? That there really is a case to be made for alternative facts? The idea of a single objective truth has never been free from controversy. Is admitting this necessarily conservative? Or liberal? Or perhaps it is a fusion, whereby largely left-wing relativist and postmodernist attacks on the idea of truth from decades ago have now simply been co-opted by right-wing political operatives.

The concept of truth in philosophy goes all the way back to Plato, who warned (through Socrates) of the dangers of false claims to knowledge. Ignorance, Socrates felt, was remediable; if one is ignorant, one can be taught. The greater threat comes from those who have the hubris to think that they already know the truth, for then one might be impetuous enough to act on a falsehood. It is important at this point to give at least a minimal definition of truth. Perhaps the most famous is that of Aristotle, who said: "to say of what is that it is not, or of what is not that it is, is false, while to say of what is that it is, and of what is not that it is not, is true."[9] Naturally, philosophers have fought for centuries over whether this sort of "correspondence" view is correct, whereby we judge the truth of a statement only by how well it fits reality. Other prominent conceptions of truth (coherentist, pragmatist, semantic) reflect a diversity of opinion among philosophers about the proper *theory* of truth, even while—as a value—there seems little dispute that truth is important.[10]

For now, however, the question at hand is not whether we have the proper theory of truth, but how to make sense of the different ways that people *subvert* truth. As a first step, it is important to acknowledge that we sometimes make mistakes and say things that are untrue without meaning to do so. In that case, one is uttering a "falsehood," as opposed to a lie, for the mistake is not intentional. The next step beyond this is "willful ignorance," which is when we do not really know whether something is true, but we say it anyway, without bothering to take the time to find out whether our information is correct. In this case, we might justifiably blame the speaker for his or her laziness, for if the facts are easily available, the person who states a falsehood seems at least partially responsible for any ignorance. Next comes lying, when we tell a falsehood with intent to deceive. This is an important milestone, for we have here crossed over into attempting to deceive another person, even though we know that what we are saying is untrue. By definition, every lie has an audience. We may not feel responsible for uttering a falsehood if no one is listening (or if we are sure that no one will believe it), but when our intent is to manipulate someone into believing something *that we know to be untrue*, we have graduated from the mere "interpretation" of facts into their falsification. Is that what post-truth is about?

The lines between the stages above are perhaps unclear and it is a slippery thing to migrate from one to another. The first time Trump said that there were no pre-inauguration conversations between his National Security Advisor and Russian officials could perhaps be attributed to willful ignorance. But when his own intelligence services then revealed that they had briefed him on exactly this—and Trump continued to deny it for *two more weeks*—one begins to infer intent. After Trump kept repeating his claim that he would have won the popular vote if not for millions of illegal ballots, the *New York Times* made the bold decision, just three days into his presidency, to print a headline saying that Trump had lied.[11]

There are other interesting relationships one can have with truth. In his delightfully brash yet rigorous book *On Bullshit*, philosopher Harry Frankfurt makes the case that when one is bullshitting, one is not necessarily lying but instead may just be demonstrating a careless indifference toward what is true. Is that what Trump is doing? And there are other, more partisan, attitudes that one can have toward truth as well. When Gingrich claims that how we feel about the murder rate is more important than FBI statistics, one suspects he is just being cynical; he is a kind of enabler for post-truth. Those political shills who "spin" the truth most favorably to their advantage, knowing full well (along with most everyone else) that this is what they are doing, are not just bullshitting, for there is clear intent to influence others. Yet post-truth also exists in an even more virulent form. This is when self-deception and delusion are involved and someone actually believes an untruth that virtually all credible sources would dispute. In its purest form, post-truth is when one thinks that the crowd's reaction actually *does* change the facts about a lie. Pundits may argue over where Trump fits into this range: whether he is a deceiver, indifferent, cynical, or delusional. Yet all seem sufficiently hostile to truth to qualify as post-truth.

As a philosopher, I cannot help but find all of these forms of post-truth deplorable. Even though it seems important to illuminate their differences and understand that there are many ways one can fit underneath the post-truth umbrella, none of this should be acceptable to those who genuinely care about the notion of truth. But the tricky part is not to explain ignorance, lying, cynicism, indifference, political spin, or even delusion. We have lived with these for centuries. Rather, what seems new in the post-truth era is a challenge not just to the idea of *knowing* reality but to the existence of reality itself. When an individual is misinformed or mistaken, he or she will likely pay the price; wishing that a new drug will cure our heart disease will not make it so. But when our leaders—or a plurality of our society—are in denial over basic facts, the consequences can be world shattering.

When South African President Thabo Mbeki claimed that antiretroviral drugs were part of a Western plot and that garlic and lemon juice could be used to treat AIDS, over 300,000 people died.[12] When President Trump maintains that climate change is a hoax invented by the Chinese government to ruin the American economy,[13] the long-term consequences may be equally devastating, if not more so. Yet the real problem here, I claim, is not merely the content of any particular (outrageous) belief, but the overarching idea that—depending on what one wants to be true—some facts matter more than others. It is not simply that climate-change deniers don't believe in facts, it's that they only want to accept those facts that justify their ideology. Like all conspiracy theorists, they feel entitled to a double standard whereby they simultaneously believe (with no evidence) that the world's climate scientists are part of a global conspiracy to hype the evidence on climate change, but then cherry pick the most favorable scientific statistics that allegedly show that the global temperature has not gone up in the last two decades.[14] Deniers and other ideologues routinely embrace an obscenely high standard of doubt toward facts that they don't want to believe, alongside complete credulity toward any facts that fit with their agenda. The main criterion is what favors their preexisting beliefs.[15] This is not the abandonment of facts, but a corruption of the process by which facts are credibly gathered and reliably used to shape one's beliefs about reality. Indeed, the rejection of this undermines the idea that *some things are true irrespective of how we feel about them*, and that it is in our best interests (and those of our policy makers) to attempt to find them.

I have previously characterized all this as a matter of "respecting truth," by embracing those methods of inquiry—like science—that have customarily led to true beliefs.[16] If someone maintains that truth does not matter, or that there is no such thing as truth, I am not sure there is much we can say to them. But is that what the post-truth phenomenon is really about? If one looks at the Oxford definition, and how all of this has played out in recent public debate, one gets the sense that post-truth is not so much a claim that truth *does not exist* as that *facts are subordinate to our political point of view*. The Oxford

Post-truth amounts to a form of ideological supremacy, whereby its practitioners are trying to compel someone to believe in something whether there is good evidence for it or not.

definition focuses on "*what*" post-truth is: the idea that feelings sometimes matter more than facts. But just as important is the next question, which is *why* this ever occurs. Someone does not dispute an obvious or easily confirmable fact for no reason; he or she does so when it is to his or her advantage. When a person's beliefs are threatened by an "inconvenient fact," sometimes it is preferable to challenge the fact. This can happen at either a conscious or unconscious level (since sometimes the person we are seeking to convince is ourselves), but the point is that this sort of post-truth relationship to facts occurs only when we are seeking to assert something that is more important to us than the truth itself. Thus post-truth amounts to a form of ideological supremacy, whereby its practitioners are trying to compel someone to believe in something whether there is good evidence for it or not. And this is a recipe for political domination.

But this perspective can and should be challenged. Do we want to live in a world where policy is made based on how it makes us feel rather than how well it will work in reality? The human animal may be wired to give some credence to our superstitions and fears, but this does not mean that we cannot train ourselves to embrace better standards of evidence. There may be legitimate theoretical questions about our ability to know objective truth, but this does not mean that epistemologists and critical theorists do not go to a physician when they get sick. Neither should governments build more prisons because they "feel" that crime is going up.

So what to do? The first step in fighting post-truth is to understand its genesis. It may seem to some commentators that the idea of post-truth simply burst onto the scene in 2016, but that is not the case. The word "post-truth" may have seen a recent uptick—as a result of Brexit and the US presidential election—but the phenomenon itself has deep roots that go back thousands of years, to the evolution of cognitive irrationalities that are shared by liberals and conservatives alike. As previously suggested, it also has roots in academic debates over the impossibility of objective truth that have been used to attack the authority of science. And all of this has been exacerbated by recent changes in the media landscape. But in trying to understand the phenomenon of post-truth we are fortunate to have a ready-made road map to guide us.

In the past two decades' explosion of science denial on topics like climate change, vaccines, and evolution, we see the birth of tactics that are now being used for post-truth. Our built-in cognitive biases, academic hair-splitting on questions about truth, and exploitation of the media have already had a prior life in the right wing's attacks on science. It's just that the battle field now encompasses all of factual reality. Before it was a dispute over a disfavored scientific theory; now it is over a photo from the US Park Service or a videotape from CNN.

Although it may seem alien and perplexing, the phenomenon of post-truth is neither opaque nor impenetrable. Yet neither is it so simple that it can be understood in a single word: Trump. In a world in which politicians can challenge the facts *and pay no political price whatsoever*, post-truth is bigger than any one person. It exists in us as well as our leaders. And the forces behind it have been building up for quite some time. This is why I believe that we have our best shot at understanding post-truth by exploring the factors that led up to it. Although the Brexit vote and the US presidential election may seem inextricably tied up with post-truth, neither was the cause of it— they were the result.

SCIENCE DENIAL AS A ROAD MAP FOR UNDERSTANDING POST-TRUTH

When the facts change I change my mind, sir. What do you do?

—John Maynard Keynes

Post-truth was foreshadowed by what has happened to science over the last several decades. Once respected for the authority of its method, scientific results are now openly questioned by legions of nonexperts who happen to disagree with them. It is important to point out that scientific results are routinely scrutinized by scientists themselves, but that is not what we are talking about here.

When a scientist puts forth a theory, it is expected that it will be put through the paces of peer review, attempts at replication, and the highest order of empirical fact checking that can be performed by one's scientific peers. The rules for this are fairly transparent, since they are in service of the scientific value that empirical evidence is paramount in evaluating the worth of a scientific theory. But mistakes can occur even with the most scrupulous safeguards in place. The process can be quite brutal, but it is necessary to make sure that, insofar as is possible, only good work gets through. Thus, failures to disclose any potential sources of bias—conflicts of interest, the source of one's funding—are taken especially seriously. Given this high level of scientific self-scrutiny, why would nonscientists feel it necessary to question the results of science? Do they really think that scientists are lax? In most cases, no; yet this is exactly the sort of claim that is routinely spread by those who find their ideological beliefs in conflict with the conclusions of science.[1] In some instances laypersons feel it is in their interest to question both the motives and the competence of scientists. And this is where "science denialism" is born.

One of the most common claims made by those who do not like some particular scientific result is that the scientists who found it were biased. At some level, one might expect that this sort of recognition of the harmful effect that nonempirical (religious, political) beliefs can have on empirical investigation would be a mark of respect for high scientific standards. Unfortunately, this is not customarily the case. In fact, it is quite common for those who oppose particular scientific findings to be quite comfortable applying their *own* ideological litmus test to an area of inquiry (even though they may deny that this is what they are doing) under the guise of "openness" and "fairness." The goal here is a cynical attempt to undercut the idea that science is fair and raise doubts that any empirical inquiry can really be value neutral. Once this has been established, it seems a small step to make the case for consideration of "other" theories. After all, if one suspects that *all* science is biased, it may not seem so egregious to consider a theory that might be tainted by one's own ideological beliefs.

Other critics, however, are a little craftier and say that selected scientists are not themselves adhering to good scientific standards: that they are being closed-minded and blind to their own self-serving interests. Some of this is based on a straightforward misunderstanding (or cynical exploitation) of how science works, based on the mistaken idea that if scientists would just gather enough evidence they could prove a theory. But this is not how science works: no matter how good the evidence, a scientific theory can never be proven true. No matter how rigorously it might have been tested, every theory is "just a theory."[2] Because of the way that scientific evidence is gathered, it is always theoretically possible that some future piece of data might come along and disprove a theory. This does not mean that scientific theories are unjustified or unworthy of belief. But it does mean that at some point scientists must admit that even their strongest explanations cannot be offered as *truth*, but only strongly warranted belief based on justification given the evidence. This alleged weakness of scientific reasoning is often exploited by those who would claim that *they* are the real scientists—that if science is an open process, then it should not be in the business of excluding alternative theories. Until a theory is absolutely proven, they believe, a competing theory could always be true.[3]

I maintain that science should not be at all embarrassed by its epistemological situation but should instead embrace it as a virtue in the search for truth. To say that a scientific theory is well warranted given the evidence is no trivial thing. Indeed, if one desires to embrace the highest standards of empirical explanation, why isn't the burden of proof on those pseudo-scientific theories that are taken to compete with scientific ones? If the "proof" game cannot be won, so we are going to play the "evidence" game instead, then where is *your* evidence, one might wish to ask the science denier. In the face of such scrutiny, denialists routinely fizzle. To those who know little or nothing about how science actually works, however, it must seem an extraordinary weakness in science—and a great opportunity for alternative theories—that they cannot "prove" evolution. (Of course, technically speaking one cannot "prove" that the world is round, either.)[4]

The most salient example of this in recent years is what has happened with climate change. Although there is virtually no scientific debate over the question of whether the global temperature is rising and humans are the primary cause of it, the public has been hoodwinked into thinking that there is a great scientific controversy over this issue. Others have told this story well elsewhere, and I will here only give a quick summary of it.[5] Instead, my goal is to show that the phenomenon of science denial in general is relevant as a way to understand the phenomenon of post-truth. But to do that we should probably start a little further back, when science denial really started to heat up in the 1950s, as tobacco companies realized that they had a vested interest in raising doubt over whether cigarette smoking caused lung cancer.

"Doubt Is Our Product"

Science denial can start from either an economic or an ideological agenda. Most commonly, it is kicked off by those who have something to lose, and is later carried on by those who get caught up in their campaign of misinformation. In his *Lies, Incorporated*, Ari Rabin-Havt deepens our understanding of this link between economic interests and post-truth politics, by considering how corporate-funded lobbying (and lying) on a range of topics has influenced political positions on climate change, guns, immigration, health care, the national debt, voter reform, abortion, and gay marriage.[6]

There are several excellent resources on the history of how science denial was born in the debate about smoking. In *Merchants of Doubt*, Naomi Oreskes and Erik Conway trace the history of how the tactics cooked up by scientists at the Tobacco Industry Research Committee (TIRC) became the blueprint for science denial.[7] The economic side of this story, as opposed to the ideological one that later arose from it, is crucial to understanding how what may seem like politically based opposition can have its roots in monetary interests. In this, it corroborates the story of how there came to be so much grass-roots push back on climate change (which was funded by oil interests). It also presages the story we will tell later about how fake news evolved from profit-seeking clickbait to full-blown disinformation.

The story begins at the Plaza Hotel in New York City in 1953. Here the heads of the major tobacco companies came together to figure out what to do in light of a devastating scientific paper that had recently been published linking cigarette tar to cancer in lab mice. The leader of the summit was John Hill, a legendary figure in public relations, who suggested that instead of continuing to fight among themselves over whose cigarettes were healthier, they needed a unified approach where they would "fight the science" by sponsoring additional "research." The executives agreed to fund this under the auspices of Hill's newly created Tobacco Industry Research Committee whose mission was to convince the public that there was "no proof" that cigarette smoking caused cancer and that previous work purporting to show such a link was being questioned by "numerous scientists."[8]

And it worked. Capitalizing on the idea that science had shown "no conclusive link" between cigarettes and cancer (for science can never do this for any two variables),[9] the TIRC took out a full-page ad in numerous American newspapers—reaching 43 million people—which had the effect of creating confusion and doubt on a scientific question that was close to settled. As Rabin-Havt puts it:

> The Tobacco Industry Research Committee was created to cast doubt on scientific consensus that smoking cigarettes causes cancer, to convince the media that there were two sides to the story about the risks of tobacco and that each side should be considered with equal weight. Finally it sought to steer politicians away from damaging the economic interests of the tobacco companies.[10]

This story continued over the next four decades—even in the face of further damning scientific research—until 1998, when the tobacco companies finally agreed to close the successor to the TIRC (and in the process disclosed thousands of internal documents which showed that they had known the truth all along) as part of a $200 billion settlement that shielded them from future lawsuits. They were then free to sell their product to a worldwide market who could be presumed to know the risks. Why did they do this? Obviously the profit made during those four decades must have far outweighed the costs incurred, but once the evidence was undeniable and the lawsuits started in earnest, the companies must have calculated that their future profits would far exceed even the $200 billion paid in settlement. Less than a decade later, the tobacco companies were found guilty of fraud under the federal racketeering (RICO) statute for conspiring to suppress what they knew about smoking and cancer as far back as 1953.[11]

As far as science denial was concerned, however, the issue was far from over, for there was now a blueprint that could be followed by others who wished to fight scientists to a standstill. In *Merchants of Doubt*, Oreskes and Conway explain this blueprint in more detail. Indeed, the authors provide evidence not only that other science deniers followed the "tobacco strategy," but also that some of the same people were involved.[12] Ever since the infamous internal memo written by a tobacco executive in 1969 which said that "doubt is our product since it is the best means of competing with the 'body of fact' that exists in the minds of the general public," it has been clear what needs to be done.[13] Find and fund your own experts, use this to suggest to the media that there are two sides to the story, push your side through public relations and governmental lobbying, and capitalize on the resulting public confusion to question whatever scientific result you wish to dispute.

As Oreskes and Conway explain, this strategy was successfully employed in later scientific "disputes" over Reagan's "Strategic Defense Initiative," nuclear winter, acid rain, the ozone hole, and global warming.[14] Some of the funding for these campaigns even came from the tobacco industry. By the time climate change became a partisan issue in the early 2000s, the mechanism of corporate-funded science denial was a well-oiled machine:

> Paid experts produced fake research that was converted into talking points and memes, then repeated on television by paid shills and spread through social media and, when necessary, hammered into the public consciousness through paid advertising campaigns.[15]

Why search for scientific disagreement when it can be manufactured? Why bother with peer review when one's opinions can be spread by intimidating the media or through public relations? And why wait for government officials to come to the "right" conclusion when you can influence them with industry money? All of this is of course shockingly cynical, yet it is only a stop on the road that today leads to post-truth. After 2016, it seems quaint to worry about leaked memos, damning testimony, and

Why search for scientific disagreement when it can be manufactured? Why bother with peer review when one's opinions can be spread by intimidating the media or through public relations? And why wait for government officials to come to the "right" conclusion when you can influence them with industry money?

videotaped contradictions when the notion of truth itself has now been thrown into question. How did anyone know that they could take things this far? Because of the success of these tactics in the next campaign: against global warming.

Climate Change and Beyond

Global warming is perhaps the most egregious case of modern science denial. As noted, there are numerous book-length works on the charade of coordinated, manufactured "skepticism" to dispute the compelling scientific evidence for anthropogenic climate change. In *Merchants of Doubt*, Oreskes and Conway make the case that a straight line can be drawn from the "tobacco strategy" of the 1950s to today's "controversy" over global warming. In this case, the funding appears to have come from the fossil fuel industry and the "think tank" in question is the Heartland Institute. It is dispiriting to learn that some of the earliest money behind Heartland came from tobacco giant Philip Morris.[16] It is perhaps less surprising to learn that some of their other funders over the years have included Exxon-Mobil and the Koch brothers:[17]

> The Heartland Institute received more than $7.3 million from Exxon Mobil between 1998 and 2010,

and nearly $14.4 million between 1986 and 2010 from foundations affiliated with Charles and David Koch, whose firm Koch Industries has substantial oil and energy holdings.[18]

Since 2008, ExxonMobil has claimed to have stopped funding all organizations that deny climate change.[19] This while investigators have turned up the fact that even while ExxonMobil was spending money to obfuscate the facts about climate change, they were making plans to explore new drilling opportunities in the Arctic once the polar ice cap had melted.[20] The Heartland Institute now warns that they will sue anyone who suggests that they are receiving current funding from fossil fuel interests. Since they have stopped disclosing the sources of their funding, one must take them at their word. What is not in dispute, however, is that Heartland embraces the *Economist*'s description of them (which appears on their website) as "the world's most prominent think tank promoting skepticism about man-made climate change."[21] Based on some leaked documents, one may also learn a bit about their strategy, which the *New York Times* describes as "to undermine the teaching of global warming in public schools [and] promote a curriculum that would cast doubt on the scientific finding that fossil fuel emissions endanger the long-term welfare of the planet."[22]

Of course, Heartland is not the only organization that disputes climate change. In the early days there were also industry-backed organizations such as the Edison Electric Group, the National Coal Association, and the Western Fuels Association, as well as industry-funded public relations organizations such as the Climate Council and the Information Council on the Environment, which seem designed to do for global warming what the TIRC had done for tobacco.[23] Until it closed in 2015, the George C. Marshall Institute also played a prominent role in generating skepticism about climate change (and also about secondhand tobacco smoke, acid rain, and the ozone hole), though in this case—despite some funding from fossil fuel interests—one suspects that their political ideology of rejecting "big-government" solutions to social problems was a key motivating force.[24] Even some university scientists (who are treated like rock stars when they come to speak at Heartland events) have raised doubts about climate change. But to claim that there is no "scientific consensus" on climate change—or that it is not "settled science"—seems a joke.

In 2004, researchers published a literature review of the then-current 928 scientific papers on climate change and found that exactly zero of them disputed the idea that anthropogenic climate change was real.[25] In a 2012 update to these findings, other researchers found that the number of dissenters was 0.17 percent out of 13,950 papers.[26]

A 2013 survey of 4,000 peer-reviewed papers that took a position on climate change found that 97 percent agreed with the position that global warming was caused by human activity.[27] Meanwhile, according to the latest public opinion poll, only 27 percent of American adults think that "almost all climate scientists agree that human behavior is mostly responsible for climate change."[28] Why would there be such widespread public confusion not simply over whether climate change is real, but over whether scientists have reached consensus on it? Because such doubt has been shamelessly manufactured over the last twenty years, by those with a financial interest in promoting it.

> In 1998, the American Petroleum Institute [API] … convened a series of meetings at its Washington, D.C., offices to discuss potential industry responses to the major climate [Kyoto Protocol] treaty being negotiated to reduce global emissions of greenhouse gases. Among the attendees were representatives from some of the country's largest oil companies, including Exxon, Chevron, and Southern Company.[29]

One wonders if the ghost of John Hill and the 1953 tobacco executives were also in attendance. The proceedings of this meeting were probably intended to be kept secret, but owing to a nearly immediate leak, the public did not this time have to wait forty years to know what had been discussed.[30] The after-action memo read in part:

Victory Will Be Achieved When

• Average citizens "understand" (recognize) uncertainties in climate science; recognition of uncertainties becomes part of the "conventional wisdom"

• Media "understands" (recognizes) uncertainties in climate science

• Media coverage reflects balance on climate science and recognition of the validity of viewpoints that challenge the current "conventional wisdom"

• Industry senior leadership understands uncertainties in climate science, making them stronger ambassadors to those who shape climate policy

• Those promoting the Kyoto treaty on the basis of extent [sic] science appears [sic] to be out of touch with reality.[31]

The similarity between the "tobacco strategy" and the API action plan is simply too strong to ignore. As one reads on in the leaked memo, one learns that important parts of the tactics for implementing this plan were to (1) "identify,

The selective use of facts that prop up one's position, and the complete rejection of facts that do not, seems part and parcel of creating the new post-truth reality.

recruit and train a team of five independent scientists to participate in media outreach," (2) "establish a Global Climate Data Center ... as a non-profit educational foundation," and (3) "inform and educate members of Congress." Does all of this sound familiar?

I believe we can stop here. Although the rest of the story is fascinating, you can turn to the resources cited throughout this chapter to tell the rest of it. The bottom line is that despite the complete disclosure of API's battle plan less than a week after it was made, it was still wildly successful. The "facts" didn't matter. The media were by now well trained to reflexively present "both sides of the story" on any "controversial" scientific issue. As a result, the public remains confused. And our new president (among other prominent Republicans such as Sen. James Inhofe and Sen. Ted Cruz) continues to proclaim that climate change is a hoax.

Implications for Post-Truth

The lesson of these cases of science denial cannot have been lost on today's politicians. Apparently one does not even have to hide one's strategy anymore. In an environment in which partisanship can be assumed, and it is often enough to "pick a team" rather than look at the evidence, misinformation can be spread in the open and fact-checking can be disparaged. The selective use of facts that prop up one's position, and the complete rejection of facts that do not, seems part and parcel of creating the new post-truth reality. It may seem unbelievable to those who care about facts and truth, but why would those who wish to achieve a political result bother with covering their tracks anymore when they pay no political price for doing so? Donald Trump surely learned this when he fomented the "birther" conspiracy for years and was then elected president. When one's supporters care more about which side you're on than what the evidence says, facts truly may be subordinate to opinions.

The tactics that we see employed in the post-truth world of today were learned in the earlier campaigns of truth deniers who wanted to fight the scientific consensus and won. And if one can deny the facts about climate change, why not those about the murder rate?[32] If the link between tobacco and cancer can be obscured by decades of misinformation and doubt, why not hope that the same could be true for any other issue that one wishes to politicize? As we can see, it is the same strategy with the same roots; it now just has a larger target, which is reality itself. In a world where ideology trumps science, post-truth is the inevitable next step.

THE ROOTS OF COGNITIVE BIAS

People can foresee the future only when it coincides with their own wishes, and the most grossly obvious facts can be ignored when they are unwelcome.

—George Orwell

One of the deepest roots of post-truth has also been with us the longest, for it has been wired into our brains over the history of human evolution: cognitive bias. Psychologists for decades have been performing experiments that show that we are not quite as rational as we think. Some of this work bears directly on how we react in the face of unexpected or uncomfortable truths.

A central concept of human psychology is that we strive to avoid psychic discomfort. It is not a pleasant thing to think badly of oneself. Some psychologists call this "ego defense" (after Freudian theory), but whether we frame it within this paradigm or not, the concept is clear. It just feels better for us to think that we are smart, well-informed, capable people than that we are not. What happens when we are confronted with information that suggests that something we believe is untrue? It creates psychological tension. How could I be an intelligent person yet believe a falsehood? Only the strongest egos can stand up very long under a withering assault of self-criticism: "What a fool I was! The answer was right there in front of me the whole time, but I never bothered to look. I must be an idiot." So the tension is often resolved by changing one of one's beliefs.

It matters a great deal, however, which beliefs change. One would like to think that it should always be the belief that was shown to be mistaken. If we are wrong about a question of empirical reality—and we are finally confronted by the evidence—it would seem easiest to bring our beliefs back into harmony by changing the one that we now have good reason to doubt. But this is not always what happens. There are many ways to adjust a belief set, some rational and some not.[1]

Three Classic Findings from Social Psychology

In 1957, Leon Festinger published his pioneering book *A Theory of Cognitive Dissonance*, in which he offered the idea that we seek harmony between our beliefs, attitudes, and behavior, and experience psychic discomfort when they are out of balance. In seeking resolution, our primary goal is to preserve our sense of self-value. In a typical experiment, Festinger gave subjects an extremely boring task, for which some were paid $1 and some were paid $20. After completing the task, subjects were requested to tell the person who would perform the task after them that it was enjoyable. Festinger found that subjects who had been paid $1 reported the task to be much more enjoyable than those who had been paid $20. Why? Because their ego was at stake. What kind of person would do a meaningless, useless task for just a dollar unless it was actually enjoyable? To reduce the dissonance, they altered their belief that the task had been boring (whereas those who were paid $20 were under no illusion as to why they had done it). In another experiment, Festinger had subjects hold protest signs for causes they did not actually believe in. Surprise! After doing so, subjects began to feel that the cause was actually a bit more worthy than they had initially thought.

But what happens when we have much more invested than just performing a boring task or holding a sign? What if we have taken a public stand on something, or even devoted our life to it, only to find out later that we've been duped? Festinger analyzed just this phenomenon in a book called *The Doomsday Cult*, in which he reported on the activities of a group called "The Seekers," who believed that their leader, Dorothy Martin, could transcribe messages from space aliens who were coming to rescue them before the world ended on December 21, 1954. After selling all of their possessions, they waited on top of a mountain, only to find that the aliens never showed up (and of course the world never ended). The cognitive dissonance must have been tremendous. How did they resolve it? Dorothy Martin soon greeted them with a new message: their faith and prayers had been so powerful that the aliens had decided to call off their plans. The Seekers had saved the world!

From the outside, it is easy to dismiss these as the beliefs of gullible fools, yet in further experimental work by Festinger and others it was shown that—to one degree or another—all of us suffer from cognitive dissonance. When we join a health club that is too far away, we may justify the purchase by telling our friends that the workouts are so intense we only need to go once a week; when we fail to get the grade we'd like in organic chemistry, we tell ourselves that we didn't really want to go to medical school anyway. But there is another aspect of cognitive dissonance that should not be underestimated, which is that such "irrational" tendencies tend to be reinforced when we are surrounded by others who believe the same thing we do. If just one person had believed in the "doomsday cult" perhaps he or she would have committed suicide or gone into hiding. But when a mistaken belief is shared by others, sometimes even the most incredible errors can be rationalized.

In his path-breaking 1955 paper "Opinions and Social Pressure," Solomon Asch demonstrated that there is a social aspect to belief, such that we may discount even the evidence of our own senses if we think that our beliefs are not in harmony with those around us. In short, peer pressure works. Just as we seek to have harmony within our own beliefs, we also seek harmony with the beliefs of those around us. In his experiment, Asch assembled seven to nine subjects, all of whom but one were "confederates" (i.e., they were "in on" the deception that would occur in the experiment). The one who was not "in on it" was the sole experimental subject, who was always placed at the last seat at the table. The experiment involved showing the subjects a card with a line on it, then another card with three lines on it, one of which was identical in length to the one on the other card. The other two lines on the second card were "substantially different" in length. The experimenter then went around the group and asked each subject to report aloud which of the three lines on the second card were equal in length to the line on the first card. For the first few trials, the confederates reported accurately and the experimental subject of course agreed with them. But then things got interesting. The confederates began to unanimously report that one of the obviously false choices was in fact equal to the length of the line on the first card. By the time the question came to the experimental subject, there was obvious psychic tension. As Asch describes it:

> He is placed in a position in which, while he is actually giving the correct answers, he finds himself unexpectedly in a minority of one, opposed by a unanimous and arbitrary majority with respect to a clear and simple fact. Upon him we have brought to bear two opposed forces: the evidence of his senses and the unanimous opinion of a group of his peers.[2]

Before announcing their answer, virtually all dissonance-primed subjects looked surprised, even incredulous. But then a funny thing happened. Thirty-seven percent of them yielded to the majority opinion. They discounted what they could see right in front of them in order to remain in conformity with the group.

Another piece of key experimental work on human irrationality was done in 1960 by Peter Cathcart Wason. In his paper "On the Failure to Eliminate Hypotheses in a Conceptual Task," Wason took the first in a number of steps to identify logical and other conceptual mistakes that humans routinely make in reasoning. In this first paper, he introduced (and later named) an idea that nearly everyone in the post-truth debate has likely heard of: confirmation bias.[3] Wason's experimental design was elegant. He gave twenty-nine college students a cognitive task whereby they would be called on to "discover a rule" based on empirical evidence. Wason presented the subjects with a three-number series such as 2, 4, 6, and said that their task would be to try to discover the rule that had been used in generating it. Subjects were requested to write down their own set of three numbers, after which the experimenter would say whether their numbers conformed to the rule or not. Subjects could repeat this task as many times as they wished, but were instructed to try to discover the rule in as few trials as possible. No restrictions were placed on the sorts of numbers that could be proposed. When they felt ready, subjects could propose their rule.

The results were shocking. Out of twenty-nine very intelligent subjects, only six of them proposed the correct rule without any previous incorrect guesses. Thirteen proposed one incorrect rule and nine proposed two or more incorrect rules. One subject was unable to propose any rule at all. What happened? As Wason reports, the subjects who failed at the task seemed unwilling to propose any set of numbers that tested the accuracy of their hypothesized rule and instead proposed only those that would confirm it. For instance, given the series 2, 4, 6, many subjects first wrote down 8, 10, 12, and were told "yes, this follows the rule." But then some just kept going with even numbers in ascending order by two. Rather than use their chance to see whether their intuitive rule of "increase by intervals of two" was incorrect, they continued to propose only confirming instances. When these subjects announced their rule they were shocked to learn that it was incorrect, even though they had never tested it with any disconfirming instances.

After this, thirteen subjects began to test their hypotheses and eventually arrived at the correct answer, which was "any three numbers in ascending order." Once they had broken out of their "confirming" mindset, they were willing to entertain the idea that there might be more than one way to get the original series of numbers. This cannot explain, however, the nine subjects who gave two or more incorrect rules, for they were given ample evidence that their proposal was incorrect, but still could not find the right answer. Why didn't they guess 9, 7, 5? Here Wason speculates that "they might not have known how to attempt to falsify a rule by themselves; or they might have known how to do it, but still found it simpler, more certain or more reassuring to get a straight answer from the experimenter."[4] In other words, at this point their cognitive bias had a firm hold on them, and they could only flail for the right answer.

All three of these experimental results—(1) cognitive dissonance, (2) social conformity, and (3) confirmation bias—are obviously relevant to post-truth, whereby so many people seem prone to form their beliefs outside the norms of reason and good standards of evidence, in favor of accommodating their own intuitions or those of their peers. Yet post-truth did not arise in the 1950s or even the 1960s. It awaited the perfect storm of a few other factors like extreme partisan bias and social media "silos" that arose in the early 2000s. And in the meantime, further stunning evidence of cognitive bias continued to come to light.

Contemporary Work on Cognitive Bias

Much has been written about the tremendous breakthroughs that have occurred in recent years in the field of behavioral economics. Borrowing a page from the earlier experimental approach of social psychologists, in the late 1970s a few economists began to question the simplifying assumptions of "perfect rationality" and "perfect information" that had always been used in neoclassical models (to make the math work right). But what if a more experimental approach could be taken?

In his book *Misbehaving: The Making of a Behavioral Economist*, Richard Thaler talks about his earliest days of collaboration with Daniel Kahneman and Amos Tversky, who were already giants in the field of cognitive psychology. In their 1974 paper "Judgment Under Uncertainty," Kahneman and Tversky took the academic world by storm, having proposed three straightforward cognitive biases of human decision making.[5] Over the next few years, their further work on choice, risk, and uncertainty revealed even more anomalies in decision making, which had such a powerful effect on other academic disciplines that in 2002 Kahneman won the Nobel Prize in Economics. (Tversky had already passed away in 1996 and was thus ineligible.) Kahneman claims never to have taken an economics course in his life and that everything he knew on the subject was due to Richard Thaler.

All of a sudden, people were paying attention to cognitive bias like never before. Part of this involved rediscovery and renewed attention to some of the facts about human psychology that were so old no one could really be sure who had first discovered them. "Source amnesia" (when we remember what we read or heard but can't remember whether it came from a reliable source) has obvious relevance to the question of how we form our beliefs. Likewise the "repetition effect" (which says that we are more likely to believe a message if it has been repeated to us many times) was well known to car salesmen and Hitler's propaganda minister alike. But along with these came fresh work that revealed a number of other built-in cognitive biases.[6] And two of the most important for our purposes build on Wason's earlier discovery of confirmation bias. These are the "backfire effect" and the "Dunning–Kruger effect," both of which are rooted in the concept of motivated reasoning.

Motivated reasoning is the idea that what we hope to be true may color our perception of what actually is true. We often reason, that is, within an emotional context. This is arguably the mechanism behind the ideas of dissonance reduction and confirmation bias, and it is easy to see why. When we feel psychic discomfort we are *motivated* to find a non-ego-threatening way to reduce it, which can lead to the irrational tendency to accommodate our beliefs to our feelings, rather than the other way around. Upton Sinclair perhaps said it best when he observed that "it is difficult to get a man to believe something when his salary depends upon him not believing it."

The idea of confirmation bias seems straightforwardly related to motivated reasoning in that it is customarily when we are *motivated* to defend the idea that one of our beliefs is right that we look for evidence to confirm it. We commonly see this mechanism at work in police detectives, who identify a suspect and then try to build a case around him, rather than search for reasons to rule him out. It is important here, however, to distinguish between motivated reasoning and confirmation bias, for they are not precisely the same thing. Motivated reasoning is a state of mind in which we find ourselves willing (perhaps at an unconscious level) to shade our beliefs in light of our opinions; confirmation bias is the mechanism by which we may try to accomplish this, by interpreting information so that it confirms our preexisting beliefs.

Some of the experimental work on motivated reasoning goes as far back as the other classic findings of social psychology. In more recent work, it has been speculated that this is why sports fans from opposing teams can look at the same piece of videotape and see different things. Let's rule out for now the idea that this sort of conclusion is reached only cynically, because we have something at stake and are not willing to admit anything that might put our team at a disadvantage. Yes, this probably does happen in some cases. There are spin doctors in sports too. We see on replay that the referees gave our football team too-favorable a spot, but why would we question that when it led to the game-winning field goal? But as any relative of a true football fall can attest, it is often the case that the rabid fan does not "see" the play in the same way others do. I live in New England, and believe me they are fighting words to maintain that Tom Brady deflated his footballs or that the New England Patriots are cheaters. And this is not just because one must always support the home team, right or wrong. New England fans truly cannot *believe* that the Patriots would be cheaters. Call it tribalism if you must, but the psychological mechanism behind it exists in all of us, Packers, Giants, or Colts fans alike.

In his work on the psychology of emotion and moral judgment, David DeSteno, a psychologist at Northeastern University, has studied the effect of such "team affiliation" on moral reasoning. In one experiment, subjects who had just met were randomly divided into teams by giving them colored wristbands. Then they were separated. The first group was told that they would be given the option of performing either a fun ten-minute task or a difficult forty-five-minute one. Each subject was then placed alone in a room and told that he or she should choose which to do—or decide by a coin flip—but that in either case the person who entered the room afterward would be left with the remaining task. What subjects didn't know is that they were being videotaped. Upon exiting the room 90 percent said that they had been fair, even though most had chosen the easier task for themselves and never bothered to flip the coin. But what is absolutely fascinating is what happened next. When the other half of the subjects were asked to watch a videotape of the liars and cheaters, they condemned them—unless they were wearing the same color wristband.[7] If we are willing to excuse immoral behavior based on something as trivial as a wristband, imagine how our reasoning might be affected if we were really emotionally committed.

Motivated reasoning has also been studied by neuroscientists, who have found that when our reasoning is colored by affective content a different part of our brain is engaged. When thirty committed political partisans were given a reasoning task that threatened their own candidate—or hurt the opposing candidate—a different part of their brain lit up (as measured by a functional-MRI scan) than when they were asked to reason about neutral content. It is perhaps unsurprising that our cognitive biases would be instantiated at the neural level, but this study provided the first experimental evidence of such differential function for motivated reasoning.[8] With this as background we are now ready to consider two of the most fascinating cognitive biases that have been used to explain how our post-truth political beliefs can affect our willingness to accept facts and evidence.

The backfire effect   The "backfire effect" is based on experimental work by Brendan Nyhan and Jason Reifler, in which they found that when partisans were presented with evidence that one of their politically expedient beliefs was wrong, they would reject the evidence and "double down" on their mistaken belief. Worse, in some cases the presentation of refutatory evidence caused some subjects to *increase* the strength of their mistaken beliefs.

In the study, subjects were given fake newspaper articles that seemed to corroborate some widely held misconceptions. In one, it supported the idea that Iraq had weapons of mass destruction (WMDs) before the Iraq War. In another, it was that President Bush had imposed a total ban on stem cell research. Both claims are factually false. When presented with corrective information—such as a quotation from a speech given by President Bush in which he admitted that there had been no WMDs in Iraq—subjects' responses broke down along partisan lines. Liberals and centrists (perhaps as expected) accepted the corrective information. Conservatives, however, did not. In fact, it was noted by the researchers that some conservative partisans actually reported becoming *more* committed to the false claim about WMDs after corrective information had been provided:

> In other words, the correction backfired—conservatives who received a correction telling them that Iraq did not have WMD were *more* likely to believe that Iraq had WMD than those in the control condition.[9]

The researchers conjectured that perhaps this result had been due to a more-heightened sense of distrust for *all* media sources among conservatives. But this did not jibe with their experimental findings, for subjects in both the correction and the no correction (control) group had read the same statement from President Bush.

> Thus the backfire effect must be the result of the experimentally manipulated correction. If subjects simply distrusted the media, they should simply ignore the corrective information. Instead, however, conservatives were found to have moved

in the "wrong" direction—a reaction that is hard to attribute to simple distrust.[10]

In a second iteration, researchers sought to test whether the same result would be true for liberal partisans. In this case, after being shown a phony news story about how Bush had imposed a total ban on stem cell research (when in fact he had only limited federal funding for stem cell lines created before August 2001 and had put no limits on privately funded research), subjects were given accurate information. In this case, the correction worked for conservatives and moderates, but not for liberals. It is important to note, however, that in this case *there was no backfire effect* for liberal partisans. While the corrective information was again "neutralized," and did not alter liberals' mistaken belief, in this instance the researchers could find no evidence that being exposed to the truth had caused liberals to *strengthen* their commitment to the false idea. The truth had not backfired.

Some have described trying to change politically salient mistaken beliefs with factual evidence as "trying to use water to fight a grease fire."[11] At least this would seem to be the case for the most partisan conservatives. As Nyhan and Reifler note in their study, however, it could hardly be true that the staunchest ideologues—of either political stripe—will *never* change their beliefs in light of factual evidence. Citing previous work on this question—and one minor result from their own study—they note that if partisans are exposed to the same discrediting information over and over again, they should become more sympathetic to corrective information. In one such study, David Redlawsk et al. consider the question of whether "motivated reasoners" ever get it, or just go on denying reality ad infinitum. Their conclusion corroborates Nyhan and Reifler's speculation: even the strongest partisans will eventually reach a "tipping point" and change their beliefs after they are continually exposed to corrective evidence.[12]

The Dunning–Kruger effect   The Dunning–Kruger effect (sometimes called the "too stupid to know they're stupid" effect) is a cognitive bias that concerns how low-ability subjects are often unable to recognize their own ineptitude. Remember that, unless one is an expert in everything, we are probably *all* prone to this effect to one degree or another. In earlier work, Kahneman and Tversky explored the sometimes frightening consequences of "overconfidence bias." Why is it that, with woefully inadequate acceptance of our perfectly predictable limitations, we decide to rent a motorized scooter when we are on vacation in Bermuda or—to choose a more famous example—decide that we have enough experience to fly a small aircraft through hazardous conditions on our way to a family wedding in Hyannisport when our flight instructor is begging us to stay on the ground? The Dunning–Kruger effect reiterates some of this, but also extends it to ask not just about the difficulty of the task at hand, but the properties of the person who is making the estimate.

In their 1999 experiment, David Dunning and Justin Kruger found that experimental subjects tended to vastly overestimate their abilities, even about subjects where they had little to no training. We are all familiar with Garrison Keillor's joke about "Lake Wobegon," a town where "all of the children are above average." But perhaps the reason this is funny is because we recognize it in ourselves. How many drivers (or lovers) would rate themselves as "below average?" Dunning and Kruger found this to extend to multiple competencies. In intelligence, humor, and even highly skilled competencies such as logic or chess, subjects tended to grossly overrate their abilities. Why is this? As the authors put it, "incompetence robs [people] of their ability to realize it. ... The skills that engender competence in a particular domain are often the very same skills necessary to evaluate competence in that domain—one's own or anyone else's."[13] The result is that many of us simply blunder on, making mistakes and failing to recognize them.

In one revealing finding, Dunning and Kruger asked forty-five intelligent undergraduates to take a twenty-item logic test from an LSAT preparation guide. As anyone familiar with the LSAT knows, these are not easy tests. Subjects were asked not only to complete the questions but to rate how they thought they had done and how this would compare to others. What researchers found was that on average students placed themselves in the 66th percentile. It is noteworthy that the students tended not to overestimate how they had done; they correctly assessed how many questions they had gotten right or wrong. Where things got out of whack was in their judgment of whether this was "above average." And in fact, the most stunning results came from those students whose performance was at the very bottom. "Although these individuals scored at the 12th percentile on average, they nevertheless believed that their general logical ability fell at the 68th percentile."[14] Perhaps this is the most shocking thing about the Dunning–Kruger result: the greatest inflation in one's assessment of one's own ability comes from the lowest performers.

At this point one is tempted to search for answers. Perhaps the students just could not admit their incompetence, so they tried to paper over it? But this seems unlikely, for when subjects were offered a $100 bonus for more accurately rating their skills, they still could not do it. What seems to be going on here is not mere deception, but self-deception. We love ourselves so much that we cannot see our own weaknesses.[15] But is it therefore any surprise that to the extent we are emotionally attached to our *political* beliefs—and in fact may even see them as part of our identity—we will be reluctant to admit that we were wrong and may even be willing to put our own "gut

Succumbing to cognitive bias can feel a lot like thinking. But especially when we are emotionally invested in a subject, all of the experimental evidence shows that our ability to reason well will probably be affected.

instinct" up against the facts of experts? When Senator James Inhofe (R-Oklahoma) brought a snowball into the US Senate Chamber in 2015 to "disprove" global warming, did he have any idea how ignorant he looked for not knowing the distinction between climate and weather? Probably not, for he was "too stupid to know he was stupid." When Donald Trump says that he knows more about ISIS than the generals do, could he really believe that?[16] Few seem willing to say "well I'm not an expert on that subject," then keep their mouths shut. Instead we soldier on and ignore the old adage about how it is "better to keep silent and be thought a fool than to open one's mouth and prove it."

Both the backfire effect and the "too stupid to know they're stupid" effect are obviously related to the phenomenon of post-truth. These and other cognitive biases not only sometimes rob us of our ability to think clearly, but inhibit our realization of when we are not doing so. Succumbing to cognitive bias can feel a lot like thinking. But especially when we are emotionally invested in a subject, all of the experimental evidence shows that our ability to reason well will probably be affected. It is a fascinating question why any of these cognitive biases might be there in the first place. Isn't truth adapative—wouldn't believing the truth increase our chances for survival?[17] For whatever reason, we must recognize that a plethora of cognitive biases are just part of the way that our brains are wired. We have no choice about whether we have them

Whether we are
liberal or conservative,
cognitive bias is part of
our human inheritance.

(even though we may hope that through careful study and training in critical reasoning we might exert some measure of control over how much we let them influence our beliefs). Whether we are liberal or conservative, cognitive bias is part of our human inheritance.

As noted, however, perhaps some cognitive biases work differently depending on our political persuasion; we have already seen that the backfire effect has less pull for liberals. Other researchers have explored the idea that there are some biases that may be purely partisan. In a fascinating paper in the journal *Psychological Science*, anthropologist Daniel Fessler has done some work on what may be called "negativity bias," which tries to explain why conservatives seem more prone to believe threatening falsehoods than liberals do.[18] In Fessler's research, he presented subjects with sixteen statements (most of which were false), but none so outlandish that they couldn't possibly be true. Some concerned innocuous content such as "exercising on an empty stomach burns more calories," while others were light-your-hair-on-fire threatening, such as "terrorist attacks in the United States have increased since September 11, 2001." He then asked subjects to self-identify as liberal or conservative, and then rate whether they thought the statements were true. There was no difference for the innocuous ones, but conservatives had a much higher probability of believing the false statements when they were threatening.[19]

Do partisans have different ways of thinking about such things? Experimental evidence has shown that the fear-based amygdala tends to be larger in conservatives than in liberals.[20] Some have speculated that this is why the lion's share of fake news stories during the 2016 election were targeted toward a conservative audience. If you are trying to sell a conspiracy theory, perhaps the right wing is more fertile ground. The negativity bias noted by Fessler was not enormous: "Using a statistical measure that gauges how widely subjects were scattered across the political spectrum, the researchers reckoned that for each tick rightward, the average subject grew 2% less skeptical of statements when they warned of bad outcomes than when they promised good ones."[21] Still, over a large enough electorate, this is perhaps enough to skew things. In any case, Fessler's work is the first to look at the question of gullibility as a function of political identity.[22]

Implications for Post-Truth

In the past, perhaps our cognitive biases were ameliorated by our interactions with others. It is ironic to think that in today's media deluge, we could perhaps be more isolated from contrary opinion than when our ancestors were forced to live and work among other members of their tribe, village, or community, who had to interact with one another to get information. When we are talking to one another, we can't help but be exposed to a diversity of views. And there is even empirical work that shows the value that this can have for our reasoning.

In his book *Infotopia*, Cass Sunstein has discussed the idea that when individuals interact they can sometimes reach a result that would have eluded them if each had acted alone.[23] Call this the "whole is more than the sum of its parts" effect. Sunstein calls it the "interactive group effect." In one study, J. C. Wason—the inventor of the term "confirmation bias" whom we met earlier in this chapter— and colleagues brought a group of subjects together to solve a logic puzzle. It was a hard one, and few of the subjects could do it on their own. But when the problem was later turned over to a group to solve, an interesting thing happened. People began to question one another's reasoning and think of things that were wrong with their hypotheses, to a degree they seemed incapable of doing with their own ideas. As a result, researchers found that in a significant number of cases a group could solve the problem even when none of its members alone could do so.[24] For Sunstein, this is key. Groups outperform individuals. And interactive, deliberative groups outperform passive ones. When we open our ideas up to group scrutiny, this affords us the best chance of finding the right answer. And when we are looking for the truth, critical thinking, skepticism, and subjecting our ideas to the scrutiny of others works better than anything else.

Yet these days we have the luxury of choosing our own selective interactions. Whatever our political persuasion, we can live in a "news silo" if we care to. If we don't like someone's comments, we can unfriend him or hide him on Facebook. If we want to gorge on conspiracy theories, there is probably a radio station for us. These days more than ever, we can surround ourselves with people who already agree with us. And once we have done this, isn't there going to be further pressure to trim our opinions to fit the group? Solomon Asch's work has already shown that this is possible. If we are a liberal we will probably feel uncomfortable if we agree with most of our friends on immigration, gay marriage, and taxes, but are not so sure about gun control. If so, we will probably pay a social price that may alter our opinions. To the extent that this occurs not as a result of critical interaction but rather a desire not to offend our friends, this is likely not to be a good thing. Call it the dark side of the interactive group effect, which any of us who has ever served on a jury can probably describe: we just feel more comfortable when our views are in step with those of our compatriots. But what happens when our compatriots are wrong? Whether liberal or conservative, none of us has a monopoly on the truth.

I am not here suggesting that we embrace false equivalence, or that the truth probably lies somewhere between

Our inherent cognitive biases make us ripe for manipulation and exploitation by those who have an agenda to push, especially if they can discredit all other sources of information.

political ideologies. The halfway point between truth and error is still error. But I am suggesting that at some level all ideologies are an enemy of the process by which truth is discovered. Perhaps researchers are right that liberals have a greater "need for cognition" than conservatives,[25] but that does not mean liberals should be smug or believe that their political instincts are a proxy for factual evidence. In the work of Festinger, Asch, and others, we can see the dangers of ideological conformity. The result is that we all have a built-in cognitive bias to agree with what others around us believe, even if the evidence before our eyes tells us otherwise. At some level we all value group acceptance, sometimes even over reality itself. But if we care about truth, we must fight against this. Why? Because the cognitive biases that I have described in this chapter are the perfect precursor for post-truth.

If we are already motivated to *want* to believe certain things, it doesn't take much to tip us over to believing them, especially if others we care about already do so. Our inherent cognitive biases make us ripe for manipulation and exploitation by those who have an agenda to push, especially if they can discredit all other sources of information. Just as there is no escape from cognitive bias, a news silo is no defense against post-truth. For the danger is that at some level they are connected. We are all beholden to our sources of information. But we are especially vulnerable when they tell us exactly what we want to hear.

THE DECLINE OF
TRADITIONAL MEDIA

Journalism is printing what someone else does not want printed: everything else is public relations.

—George Orwell

It is no secret that one of the recent facilitators of the "information silo"—which has fed our built-in predilection for confirmation bias—is the rise of social media. That story cannot be told, though, without first coming to grips with the decline of traditional media.

In its heyday, what is today called the American "prestige press" (the *New York Times*, the *Washington Post*, the *Los Angeles Times*, and the *Wall Street Journal*) and network television (ABC, CBS, and NBC) were the main sources for news. "In 1950, the average daily total paid circulation for U.S. daily newspapers was 53.8 million (equivalent to 123.6 per cent of households)."[1] Think about that for a minute. That is over 100 percent. So some households were subscribing to not one but *two* newspapers. "By 2010, the average daily total paid circulation of U.S. daily newspapers was about 43.4 million (equivalent to 36.7 per cent of households)." Think about that too; that means a loss of readership of almost 70 percent. Over at the television networks, since the 1950s the news has been delivered each evening by an anchorman for half an hour on a nationwide broadcast.[2] Walter Cronkite sat at the big desk at CBS from 1962 to 1981 and was often cited as "the most trusted man in America."

Many think of this as the "golden age" for news. Throughout the 1950s and 1960s, the competition from TV networks had caused many smaller newspapers to go out of business. This "left most major American cities with a de facto monopoly paper, one which was better, richer, and more serious than those papers that had existed some twenty years earlier."[3] And on television? Because they were expected to broadcast only half an hour of news a day, the networks could put most of their effort into investigative reporting. Other than the occasional (and terrifying) alerts saying "we interrupt this broadcast to bring you a special bulletin" that portended war or assassination, the news was confined to its own niche, so that TV stations could profit from their entertainment programming.

Although there wasn't much news on TV, this turned out to be a blessing for the news divisions, because they were not expected to make any money. Ted Koppel explains:

Network executives were afraid that a failure to work in the "public interest, convenience and necessity," as set forth in the Radio Act of 1927, might cause the Federal Communications Commission to suspend or even revoke their licenses. The three major networks pointed to their news divisions (which operated at a loss or barely broke even) as evidence that they were fulfilling the FCC's mandate. News was, in a manner of speaking, the loss leader that permitted NBC, CBS and ABC to justify the enormous profits made by their entertainment divisions.[4]

This began to change with the appearance of the CBS news show *60 Minutes* in 1968, which (after its first three years) became the first news show in history to turn a profit. Suddenly a lightbulb went on at the networks. Although it did not change the model or expectations for TV news immediately, network executives began to see that news could be profitable.[5]

Still, the golden age of broadcasting persisted right through the 1970s, but then the Iran hostage crisis of 1979 led to a conundrum. The public was suddenly hungry for more news, but how could this be accommodated without disrupting the hugely profitable entertainment broadcasts? Johnny Carson's *Tonight Show* over at NBC was a beast. CBS had all but given up by running a late movie during that time slot. ABC was running prime time reruns. Then someone had an idea:

> The ABC television network at the time decided to try something different by moving the daily Iran briefing to the late evening. This was also a marketing decision: ABC had no late-night programming against Johnny Carson's venerable talk show on its rival NBC, and news programming was, by comparison, cheap. ABC filled the evening slot with a new program called *Nightline* devoted solely to coverage of the [hostage] crisis. Each night, ABC would splash the screen with "America Held Hostage," followed by the number of days of captivity. The anchor (usually the veteran ABC newsman Ted Koppel) would then fill the time by interviewing experts, journalists, and other figures associated with the crisis.[6]

This was very successful, and the program survived long after the end of the hostage crisis a year later. But still the question remained: would anyone want to watch more news than that?

Next into the pool was CNN in 1980, which was something of a gamble. All of a sudden there would be twenty-four hours of news programming to fill. Whereas Koppel could parade a stream of experts to talk about Iran, how many experts were there and on how many newsworthy topics? On the viewer's side, would they be willing to treat the news as a twenty-four-hour buffet and graze in and out whenever they felt like it, rather than waiting for the next edition of the newspapers or their "evening meal" broadcast with the network anchors? Were they ever. Although CNN was criticized for providing "watered down" coverage as compared with the broadcast networks, it was almost immediately a success. In 1983, a *New York Times* business section story reported on CNN's first profits.[7] Throughout the 1980s and beyond, CNN's viewership grew, as a series of crises drew people to cable news: the *Challenger* space shuttle blew up, Tiananmen Square happened, the Berlin Wall came down, and finally there was the Gulf War.[8]

Of course, there were also complaints about bias, but these had been a persistent theme for decades for newspapers, broadcast, and cable news alike. Lyndon Johnson hated the coverage that the networks gave him during the Vietnam era. Nixon's vice president Spiro Agnew dismissed the Washington press corps as "nattering nabobs of negativism." There were eternal rumblings from the right that the news reflected a persistently "liberal bias," but there was really no alternative until the late 1980s.

Talk radio had already been on the air for thirty years before Rush Limbaugh came along, but, as Tom Nichols explains in his book *The Death of Expertise*, Limbaugh did something new: "[he set] himself up as a source of truth in opposition to the rest of American media."[9] Feeling that the rest of the media was "in the tank" for liberals like Bill Clinton, Limbaugh sought to give voice to the rest of America. And he was wildly successful.

> Within a few years of his first broadcast, Limbaugh was heard on more than six hundred stations nationwide. ... [Limbaugh] built a loyal national base of followers by allowing them to call in and express their support. The calls were screened and vetted; according to a manager at one of Limbaugh's early affiliates, this was because Limbaugh felt that he was not very good at debate. Debate, however, was not the point: the object was to create a sense of community among people who already were inclined to agree with each other.[10]

People listened to Limbaugh's show not to learn new "facts," but because they felt alienated from what they perceived to be the political bias of the news coverage they were getting from newspapers and TV. And besides, until the debut of call-in radio, the media had always been unidirectional: someone else was telling them what was true.

Limbaugh's show allowed people to have their own voices heard and participate in a community. Before anyone in the media was even talking about confirmation bias, Rush Limbaugh had already discovered it. And it made him a juggernaut.

By now, others were realizing the potential market share for partisan news coverage. MSNBC was founded in July 1996. Fox News came soon after in October 1996. Both saw themselves as alternatives to CNN. You will find people to this day who are unwilling to accept that MSNBC is partisan. In its first few years, it was decidedly less so, featuring conservative commentators like Ann Coulter and Laura Ingraham as regular contributors. At some point, however, MSNBC settled into its own (sometimes uncomfortable) niche for a liberal perspective on the news. Fox News—which was the creation of conservative media consultant Roger Ailes—displayed no such ambivalence:

The arrival of Fox was, in its way, the ultimate expression of the partisan division in how people seek out sources of news in a new electronic marketplace. What Limbaugh tried to do with radio … Ailes made a reality with a network. Had Ailes not created Fox, someone would have, because the market, as talk radio proved, was already there. As the conservative author and Fox commentator

Charles Kruthammer likes to quip, Ailes "discovered a niche audience: half the American people."[11]

Fox has taken partisan news coverage to a new level. The day after the tragic shooting of twenty elementary school students in Newtown, Connecticut, Fox News executives sent a directive to their producers not to allow anyone to discuss gun control on the air.[12] The practice of Fox executives seeking to slant the day's news toward conservative talking points was in fact well known.[13] This cannot help but affect news content. A 2013 study found that 69 percent of Fox News guests were skeptical of climate change, compared to 29 percent in the *Los Angeles Times* and 17 percent in the *Washington Post*.[14] Another study found that 68 percent of Fox News stories reflected personal opinions, compared to only 4 percent at CNN.[15] As a result, with no discernible line drawn between hard news and partisan opinion, hard-core Fox News viewers can perhaps be forgiven for believing and spreading some of the misinformation they have learned. Indeed, one 2011 study found that Fox News viewers were *less well informed* than those who did not watch any news.[16]

Ted Koppel has in recent years cast himself as a staunch opponent of this kind of partisan media—whether from the left or the right—and argues that it is a danger to our democracy. It is perhaps ironic that his show

Nightline in the 1980s was one of the first to demonstrate the economic potential of interview-based news coverage, but Koppel nonetheless feels that things have now gone too far:

> The commercial success of both Fox News and MSNBC is a source of nonpartisan sadness for me. While I can appreciate the financial logic of drowning television viewers in a flood of opinions designed to confirm their own biases, the trend is not good for the republic. … Beginning, perhaps, from the reasonable perspective that absolute objectivity is unattainable, Fox News and MSNBC no longer even attempt it. They show us the world not as it is, but as partisans (and loyal viewers) at either end of the political spectrum would like it to be. This is to journalism what Bernie Madoff was to investment: He told his customers what they wanted to hear, and by the time they learned the truth, their money was gone.[17]

Since Trump's election, Koppel has trained his sights more specifically on Fox. In a recent interview with Sean Hannity from Fox News, the two had this exchange:

> **HANNITY** We have to give some credit to the American people that they are somewhat intelligent and

that they know the difference between an opinion show and a news show. You're cynical.

KOPPEL I am cynical.

HANNITY Do you think we're bad for America? You think I'm bad for America?

KOPPEL Yeah … in the long haul I think you and all these opinion shows—

HANNITY Really? That's sad, Ted. That's sad.

KOPPEL No, you know why? Because you're very good at what you do, and because you have attracted a significantly more influential—

HANNITY You are selling the American people short.

KOPPEL No, let me finish the sentence before you do that.

HANNITY I'm listening. With all due respect. Take the floor.

KOPPEL You have attracted people who are determined that ideology is more important than facts.[18]

Some are willing to dismiss the entire work product of Fox News as the godfather of "fake news." (One does not have to listen long to criticism of the network to hear some wag make the too-easy joke that it should really be called "Faux News.") The problem of "fake news" and its relationship to the post-truth phenomenon is an enormous topic that we'll discuss in the next chapter. I bring it up now only because some commentators have claimed that "fake news" started not with Fox but with satire.

In a 2014 Pew survey that asked Americans to name their "most trusted" news source, there was a predictable partisan split. Among self-identified conservatives, Fox News led with 44 percent. With liberals, it was network broadcast news at 24 percent and a more or less three-way tie for second place between public television, CNN, and … Jon Stewart's *The Daily Show*.[19] But wait. *The Daily Show* is *comedy*. Before he retired as "anchor" of *The Daily Show* in 2015, Jon Stewart himself said that he reported "mock" news. His job was to get laughs, not dig for facts. Amid growing concern by "real" news people during his tenure that many young people were nonetheless getting their news from his show, Stewart defended himself by saying "if your idea of confronting me is that I don't ask hard-hitting enough news questions, we're in bad shape, fellows."[20]

Others are not willing to let Stewart, or Andy Borowitz at the *New Yorker*, or *The Onion*, off so easily. In a recent op-ed in the *Los Angeles Times* entitled "The Left Has a Post-Truth Problem Too: It's Called Comedy," Stephen Marche argued that "the post-truth condition, in which Trumpism has flourished, has its roots in left-wing satire.

… In 2009, a *Time* magazine poll declared [Jon] Stewart the most trusted news anchor on the air."[21] But I would argue that this is not a fair interpretation. Satire is a long-standing foil to the lies and bullshit that politicians try to get us to accept as truth. It is not intended to be taken for the real thing. That is in part its point. By making fun of reality, satire intends to highlight the absurdity in real life. If one accepted satire as real, the point would be lost. The intention of satire is not to deceive, but to ridicule. As Marche himself notes in his piece, "in one sense … political satire is the opposite of fake news. Satirists rip away the pretenses of journalism to reveal what they believe to be true. Fake news sites use the pretenses of journalism to spread what they know to be false."[22] Yet Marche argues that despite their differing intentions, the result is the same: "Political satirists, and their audiences, have turned the news itself into a joke. No matter what the content of their politics, they have contributed to the post-factual state of American political discourse."[23]

This seems a heavy burden to lay at the feet of political satire. Yet one hears an echo of Hannity's defense of Fox News: "We have to give some credit to the American people that they are somewhat intelligent and that they know the difference between an opinion show and a news show." Is the messenger responsible for any false impressions that may be created in his or her community of followers? Or should that responsibility rest only with those who intend to mislead people into believing something that is untrue? But what if the way the story is told has a role in creating those misconceptions? Is shifting the burden of responsibility back to one's audience enough to absolve one of bias?

The Problem of Media Bias

We have already seen how the traditional media declined in competitive terms once a more partisan opinion-based model grew up to challenge it. What I would like to address now is whether it also declined in its quality and commitment to the values of good journalism.

With the rise of cable TV "news" shows in 1996, many in the traditional media began to blanch. They did not want to be confused with *that*! Thus, in both network TV coverage, on CNN, and in the "prestige press" newspapers, they sought to distinguish themselves by placing even more emphasis on "objectivity." The Fox News slogan of "fair and balanced" coverage was surely intended to mock the traditional news media. It's not that Fox probably saw their own coverage as any more balanced; rather, they thought that they *were* the balance. The other media were too far left, so they balanced things out on the right. But since the traditional media could never accept the idea that they *were* actually biased toward the left, they resolved to show that they really *could* be "fair and balanced" in their

Is the messenger responsible for any false impressions that may be created in his or her community of followers? Or should that responsibility rest only with those who intend to mislead people into believing something that is untrue?

own coverage, so they started to report "both sides" of any controversial issues.

Far from increasing objectivity, this had the ironic effect of lowering their commitment to providing accurate news coverage. In an environment in which partisans are desperate to get their story out, one does not succeed in upholding the highest standards of journalistic integrity (the most important of which should be telling the truth) by giving partisan shills a platform to air their grievances. Yet this is exactly what happened. The mantra of objectivity was reflected in a resolve to provide "equal time" and a reflex to "tell both sides of the story" even on factual matters. While this may have been a reasonable or even laudable goal when it came to opinion-based topics, it proved to be a disaster for science coverage. By allowing "equal time," the media only succeeded in creating "false equivalence" between two sides of an issue even when there were not really two credible sides.

We have already seen in chapter 2 how science deniers have figured out how to exploit media worries about objectivity. No longer do they need to take out full-page ads to get their story out. All they have to do is bully the media into believing that if "other research" exists on scientific topics but they aren't covering it, it must be because they are biased. Journalists took the bait and started to cover both sides of "controversial" issues like climate change and vaccines, even if the controversy had been generated only

By allowing "equal time," the media only succeeded in creating "false equivalence" between two sides of an issue even when there were not really two credible sides.

by those who had something financial or political at stake. And the consequence for the general public was utter confusion over what amounted to a media-abetted campaign of disinformation.

In 1988, President George H. W. Bush promised to fight the "greenhouse effect" with the "White House effect" long before climate change became a political issue.[24] Over the next few years, however, global warming became deeply partisan. The oil companies had started doing their own "research," and they wanted the media to cover it. Simultaneously, they were contributing money to and lobbying government officials. We now understand that all of this was merely "manufactured doubt" meant to obscure the fact that the world's climate scientists had all but reached consensus on the fact that climate change was occurring and that human activity was responsible for it. But too much money was at stake to let this issue be left to the scientists. And as long as there were "skeptics" out there, the media felt duty-bound to report climate change as a disputed topic.

James Hansen was one of the earliest whistle blowers on the subject of climate change. In 1988, he gave testimony before Congress that resulted in two bills before the US Senate. As the former head of NASA's Goddard Institute for Space Studies, he is one of the world's leading experts on this subject. Yet consider below his first-hand account of the indignity he suffered in the face of the media's mandate for "objectivity" about a factual subject:

> I used to spread the blame uniformly until, when I was about to appear on public television, the producer informed me that the program "must" also include a "contrarian" who would take issue with claims of global warming. Presenting such a view, he told me, was a common practice in commercial television as well as radio and newspapers. Supporters of public TV or advertisers, with their own special interests, require "balance" as a price for their continued financial support. Gore's book reveals that while more than half of the recent newspaper articles on climate change have given equal weight to such contrarian views, virtually none of the scientific articles in peer-reviewed journals have questioned the consensus that emissions from human activities cause global warming. As a result, even when the scientific evidence is clear, technical nit-picking by contrarians leaves the public with the false impression that there is still great scientific uncertainty about the reality and causes of climate change.[25]

What happened to Hansen, moreover, was not at all atypical. Overnight, the public was treated to split-screen TV "debates" with scientists on one side and "skeptics" on the other. The host would let them both talk for roughly the same amount of time, then pronounce the issue "controversial." For a while, most of the TV news shows seemed to be emulating the Fox News slogan "we report, you decide."

Naturally, the public was confused. Was there a scientific controversy over climate change or not? If not, why were the TV shows presenting it as if there were one? The media may have told themselves that it was not their job to take a stand on a "partisan" issue, but in an environment in which a little research surely would have told them that scientists were *not* divided, this amounted to journalistic malpractice. The goal of objectivity is not to give equal time between truth and falsehood—it is to facilitate the truth. Since scientists had already reached a consensus on climate change, the only "controversy" afoot was a political one that had been stirred up by the oil companies and those who believed their lies. The upshot is that even though there was no actual scientific controversy—just as forty years before there had been none over the link between smoking and cancer—the public thought that there was one.

And who can blame them? They saw it on the news! By now the media had abandoned its job of "telling the truth" in favor of "covering their ass" by showing that they were not biased, which played right into the hands of those who were seeking to create confusion on factual matters through nothing more than bogus skepticism. Why did the media allow it? In part, it may have been due to lazy reporting. As one commentator put it:

> Objectivity excuses lazy reporting. If you're on deadline and all you have is "both sides of the story," that's often good enough. It's not that such stories laying out the parameters of a debate have no value for our readers but too often, in our obsession with ... "the latest," we fail to push the story, incrementally, toward a deeper understanding of what is true and what is false.[26]

But this can have horrible consequences, for if you provide a counternarrative of falsehood to something that is true, it allows motivated reasoning to take root. Political shills were exploiting the media, and the media were misleading their viewers. But there is another angle as well: profit. In an increasingly competitive media environment, networks may have been looking for a "story," which required some degree of drama. If there is one true thing that Donald Trump said in his book *The Art of the Deal* it is that the media loves controversy more than truth.[27] How can one justify such an accusation rather than conclude that it was all just an anomaly about an admittedly complex subject? Because it happened again, on the subject of the alleged link between vaccines and autism, based on the bogus research of Dr. Andrew Wakefield in 1998.

Here the drama was even higher. Sick kids and their grieving parents! Hollywood celebrities taking sides! Maybe a conspiracy and a governmental cover-up! And again, the media failed utterly to report the most likely conclusion based on the evidence: Wakefield's research was almost certainly bogus. He had a massive undisclosed conflict of interest, his research was unreproducible, and his medical license had been revoked. This was all known in 2004, at the height of the vaccine-autism story. Later, when definitive word came out that Wakefield's research had been a fraud and a hoax, the damage had already been done. Years of split-screen TV debates had taken their toll. Vaccination rates had plummeted and what had once been a nearly eradicated disease—the measles—later had an outbreak among eighty-four people across fourteen states.[28]

If you think that the print media were blameless in all this, you would be mistaken. In a 2004 study entitled "Balance as Bias: Global Warming and the US Prestige Press," Maxwell Boykoff and Jules Boykoff found that the norm of "balanced reporting" had caused the *New York Times*, the *Washington Post*, the *Los Angeles Times*, and the *Wall Street Journal* to seriously mislead the public on climate change.[29] The problem here was not any so-called political bias. It was instead what the researchers call "information bias," which is when the news gathering and reporting routines of journalists result in coverage that is distorted from the truth. In short, "[information] bias is the divergence of prestige-press global-warming coverage from the general consensus of the scientific community."[30] But how could this happen? How could it be that adhering to the journalistic values of objectivity, fairness, accuracy, and balance could lead one *away* from the truth? The answer lies in succumbing to the pressure to achieve "balanced reporting" by including information provided by partisans who have a stake in pushing the reporter toward something other than the truth. This creates a "denial discourse" that can give undue credibility to fringe opinions: "Balanced reporting has allowed a small group of global warming skeptics to have their views amplified."[31] The problem is really quite simple. If you make a recipe with just one rotten ingredient, the whole dish will taste rotten.

> Balance aims for neutrality. It requires that reporters present the views of legitimate spokespersons of the conflicting sides in any significant dispute, and provide both sides with roughly equal attention.[32]

But there is a danger because balance is often a substitute for fact-checking:

> The typical journalist, even one trained as a science writer, has neither the time nor the expertise to check the validity of claims himself.[33]

Thus, the situation is ripe for exploitation by ideological "experts" who have a stake in how a particular scientific issue gets reported.

Did this happen with the issue of global warming? It should be no surprise that it did. Remember that 1998 meeting convened by the American Petroleum Institute and their strategy memo that got leaked afterward? Those "independent scientists" that the oil companies recruited paid off. Boykoff and Boykoff explicitly refer to the success of the API's media strategy as a factor in creating media bias in climate change coverage:

> In the majority of coverage in the US prestige press, balanced accounts prevailed; these accounts gave "roughly equal attention" to the view that humans were contributing to global warming, and the other view that exclusively natural fluctuations could explain the earth's temperature increase.[34]

The print journalists got played, just as the TV journalists had.

Implications for Post-Truth

The guardians of traditional journalistic values are in something of a no-win situation these days. As they watch their market share erode in the face of the increasing popularity of opinion-based, sometimes unedited, content they are taken to task for being biased even when they are doing their best to uphold the truth. If they call the president a liar (even when he is lying), they are criticized. If they disregard the contribution of "skeptics" on scientific debates, they are accused of telling only one side of the story. Is it any wonder that some in the mainstream press and television networks wish they could go back to the "good old days" when journalistic values were championed and their authority was respected?[35]

What they get instead is an onslaught of criticism. Donald Trump has taken to calling any media report he does not like "fake news." In his campaign rallies he called the press "among the most dishonest people on earth."[36] And it is working. In the latest Gallup poll it was reported that Americans' trust in the mass media has now sunk to a new low: from a high of 72 percent in 1976 in the immediate aftermath of the Watergate crisis and Vietnam, it has now dropped to 32 percent.[37]

This is all just another step on the road to post-truth. Since the audience for news now consists of so many partisans, the line between traditional and alternative media has blurred, and many now prefer to get their news from sources that adhere to questionable values for truth telling. Indeed, many cannot even tell these days which sources are biased. And if one believes that all media are biased, perhaps it makes less difference to choose an information source that is biased in one's favor. Those who have provided charts that attempt to measure the reliability of various media sources since the election have been met with threats of bodily harm.[38]

The rise of social media has of course facilitated this informational free-for-all. With fact and opinion now presented side by side on the Internet, who knows what to believe anymore? With no filters and no vetting, readers and viewers these days are readily exposed to a steady stream of pure partisanship. With the reputation of the mainstream media at its nadir, those with a stake in distributing propaganda no longer need worry about getting others to tell *their* side of the story anymore. Now they have their own media outlets.

And if that fails, there is always Twitter. If the media is the enemy, then Trump can get his message directly to the people. Who needs fact-checking when people can hear directly from the president of the United States?

The challenge to reality is complete.

THE RISE OF SOCIAL MEDIA AND THE PROBLEM OF FAKE NEWS

Don't believe everything you read on the Internet.

—Thomas Jefferson

Unsurprisingly, the decline of traditional media has been in large part a result of the Internet. The peak year for print newspaper circulation in the United States was 1984.[1] Then began a long slide due in part to losing market share to cable TV, but things really began to crumble with the large-scale public availability of the World Wide Web in the 1990s. When the financial crisis hit in 2008, many newspapers began a self-stoking cycle: revenues fell, they cut back staff, their product shrank, and subscribers continued to flee.

> Analysts have warned in recent years that by offering steadily less in print, newspapers were inviting

readers to stop buying. Most papers have sharply reduced their physical size—fewer and smaller pages, with fewer articles—and the newsroom staffs that produce them. "It just seems impossible to me that you're cutting costs dramatically without having some impact on the editorial quality of your product," said Peter Appert, an analyst at Goldman Sachs. "I can't prove that this is driving circulation, but it's certainly something that if I were a newspaper publisher would keep me up at night."[2]

In the most recent Pew Research Center "State of the News Media" report from 2016, they give the full nightmare:

> For newspapers, 2015 might as well have been a recession year. Weekday circulation fell 7% and Sunday circulation fell 4%, both showing their greatest declines since 2010. At the same time, advertising revenue experienced its greatest drop since 2009, falling nearly 8% from 2014 to 2015. … In 2014, the latest year for which data were available, newsroom employment also declined 10%, more than in any other year since 2009. The newspaper workforce has shrunk by about 20,000 position, or 39%, in the last 20 years.[3]

Meanwhile, over at the broadcast and cable TV networks, they were experiencing decline of another sort. In the last chapter we saw that the process of forsaking fact-based investigative reporting for opinion-based pundit-driven coverage had already begun as early as the 1990s. The TV networks (along with newspapers) had already been scaling back or closing their foreign news bureaus for years, in favor of cheaper, domestic coverage.[4] By 2015—at least from a financial and ratings perspective—that looked like a prescient decision, as the biggest news story in decades was happening right here at home.

To say that the 2016 presidential election was a boon for the TV networks would be a vast understatement. Their viewership exploded and the profits began to roll in. CNN reported $1 billion in gross profit for 2016, the best year in its history.[5] Over at Fox (which was already the most profitable cable network) they were projected to make $1.67 billion.[6] Day and night, the public just couldn't get enough election coverage. "Year over year, daytime viewership grew by 60% for Fox, 75% for CNN, and a remarkable 83% for MSNBC."[7] How did they do that? In large part, by giving the people what they wanted—and that turned out to be saturation coverage of Donald Trump. Fox News, of course, was happy to shill for Trump; some were already dismissing their coverage as nothing more than propaganda for the Republican party.[8] But even at CNN, they ran Trump's rallies live and in full, with no vetting or editorial comment. By some estimates, the cable news networks gave Trump nearly $5 billion in free media during the 2016 election.[9] But of course, it was in their self-interest to do so. Trump was the golden goose, and even while he profited by their coverage, the TV networks benefited as well. Did they let this cloud their responsibility to check some of Trump's lies? Many think they did, as few networks applied any higher standard of truth telling than the "false equivalence" tactic they had already used on scientific topics, whereby they included both Trump and Clinton supporters on their pundit panels. Some would go so far as to say that CNN helped to get Donald Trump elected president.[10] CNN President Jeff Zucker won't go this far, but even he admits that "if we made any mistake last year, it's that we probably did put on too many of his [Trump's] campaign rallies in those early months and let them run."[11] Meanwhile during those rallies Trump was insulting the media at every turn. He put them in fenced pens and forbade them from taking cutaway shots of the crowd during his speeches. How did he achieve that? The news networks agreed to it, as a condition of enjoying the Trump bonanza. With newspapers on life support, and TV news all but in the tank at least for their own self-interest, where could the public go to vent their frustrations at the latest media-enabled outrage or get the straight dope from people they trusted? Straight to social media.

When it was created in 2004, Facebook was a social networking site that allowed users to connect with their existing friends and make new ones. They could share their thoughts and participate in an online community on whatever topic they liked. As it grew, Facebook gained strength as a news aggregator. This occurred not merely through people sharing news stories on their own pages, but also in the "trending stories" column on the right side of the page that was curated (and edited) by Facebook. This was driven by "likes," so it targeted and displayed news stories we would be more likely to want to see. Naturally other companies wanted to get into the act, not only of presenting user content but of creating an alternative network for news stories that had accreted from other sources. YouTube was founded in 2005 and Twitter in 2006.

The rise of social media as a source of news blurred the lines even further between news and opinion, as people shared stories from blogs, alternative news sites, and God knows where, as if they were all true. As the 2016 presidential election heated up, more and more content on social media skewed partisan, which fit well with a "motivated reasoning" vibe enabled by technology. We could click on "news" stories that told us what we wanted to hear (whether they had been vetted for accuracy or not) as opposed to some of the factual content from mainstream media that may have been less palatable. Without knowing that they were doing so, people could feed their desire for confirmation bias (not to mention score some free news content) directly, without bothering to patronize traditional news sources. Why pay for a newspaper subscription when you could get as many stories as you wanted from friends that had just as much to say about the events you were interested in? The "prestige press" didn't stand a chance.

In a recent Pew poll, 62 percent of US adults reported getting their news from social media, and 71 percent of *that* was from Facebook. This means that *44 percent of the total adult US population* now gets its news from Facebook.[12] This reflects a sea change in the source (and composition) of our news content. With the decline in vetting and editing, how are we supposed to know anymore which stories are reliable? While traditional news is still out there, it's getting harder and harder to tell what is a well-sourced, fact-driven piece and what is not. And of course some people just prefer to read (and believe) news that already fits their point of view anyway.

The result is the well-known problem of "news silos" that feed polarization and fragmentation in media content.[13] If we get our news from social media, we can tune out those sources we don't like, just as we can unfriend people who disagree with our political opinions. Whether our news feeds are reliable or fact free will depend on vetting by our friends and the algorithm that Facebook uses to decide which news stories we will "like" more than others. How ironic that the Internet, which allows for immediate access to reliable information by anyone who bothers to look for it, has for some become nothing but an echo chamber. And how dangerous. With no form of editorial control over what is now sometimes presented as "news," how can we know when we are being manipulated?

When I was about seven years old, I remember going to the local supermarket with my mom and standing in the checkout line. There I saw some sensational newspaper headline. I pointed it out to my mom, who said "Oh that's trash. That's the *National Enquirer*. They print all sorts of lies. You can't believe that." We then launched into an earnest conversation about how she could know it wasn't true without even reading the story and how a newspaper could get away with printing something it knew was false. The *National Enquirer* still exists in paper form at the checkout line, so I ask you to imagine a twenty-first-century thought experiment. Suppose you brought home a copy of the *National Enquirer* and the *New York Times* and cut out the news stories with scissors. Then you placed them side by side in a collage, scanned them into an electronic format, and corrected the font so that you couldn't immediately tell which one was which. How would you know at a glance which stories were true? But this is exactly how our news is presented to us now on news aggregator websites like Facebook, Google, and Yahoo. You might say that you'd look at the source of the story, but do you know

How ironic that the Internet, which allows for immediate access to reliable information by anyone who bothers to look for it, has for some become nothing but an echo chamber.

which sources are reliable? If you see the *New York Times* you might be more inclined to trust it. But what if it says InfoWars? Or Newsmax? Or ABCNews.com.co?

There are so many "news" sources these days that it is nearly impossible to tell which of them are reliable and which are not without some careful vetting. Then there is the problem that some of the sources have taken on clever disguises to try to make themselves look as legitimate as possible. Is ABCNews.com.co a part of ABC News? It is not. With the presentation of traditionally vetted, fact-checked stories right alongside lies and propaganda, how can one tell what is true anymore? Indeed, what a perfect storm for the exploitation of our ignorance and cognitive biases by those with an agenda to put forward.

The History of Fake News

Fake news did not begin with the 2016 presidential election, nor with the invention of social media. Indeed, some have held that fake news was invented right along with the concept of "news" itself.

> Fake news took off at the same time that news
> began to circulate widely, after Johannes Gutenberg
> invented the printing press in 1439. "Real" news
> was hard to verify in that era. There were plenty of

news sources—from official publications by political and religious authorities, to eyewitness accounts from sailors and merchants—but no concept of journalistic ethics or objectivity. Readers in search of fact had to pay close attention. … [Fake news] has been around … a lot longer, in fact, than verified "objective" news, which emerged in force a little more than a century ago.[14]

Fake news continued down through the ages, even during the scientific revolution and the Enlightenment. Just before the French Revolution, a number of pamphlets appeared in Paris recounting the near-bankruptcy of the government. These were put out, however, by rival political factions, who used different numbers and blamed different people. Finally, enough information came out that people began to get the true picture, "but, like today, readers had to be both skeptical and skilled to figure out the truth."[15] During the American Revolution, fake news appeared by both the British and the Americans, including Benjamin Franklin's pure fiction that some of the "scalping" Indians were working alongside King George.[16]

Fake news continued in America as elsewhere long after that, but finally a standard of "objectivity" began to emerge. According to Michael Schudson, in his wonderfully clear and insightful book *Discovering the News: A Social History of American Newspapers*:

Before the 1830s, objectivity was not an issue. American newspapers were expected to present a partisan viewpoint, not a neutral one. Indeed, they were not expected to report the "news" of the day at all in the way we conceive of it— the idea of "news" itself was invented in the Jacksonian era.[17]

What happened during the Jackson era that led to the idea of nonpartisan, strictly factual news?

This has to do with the rise of the first American wire service, the Associated Press. The telegraph was invented in the 1840s, and, to take advantage of its speed in transmitting news, a group of New York newspapers organized the Associated Press in 1848. Since the Associated Press gathered news for publication in a variety of papers with widely different political allegiances, it could only succeed by making its reporting "objective" enough to be acceptable to all its members and clients. By the late nineteenth century, the AP dispatches were markedly more free from editorial comment than most reporting for single newspapers. It has been argued, then, that the practice of the Associated Press became the ideal of journalism in general.[18]

This did not mean that fake news disappeared, or even that single newspapers were more "objective." The Associated Press may have given them the raw material to be more nonpartisan, but individual newspapers continued to do as they wished.

> Objective reporting did not become the chief
> norm or practice in journalism in the late
> nineteenth century when the Associated Press was
> growing. ... At the turn of the century there was
> as much emphasis in leading papers on telling a
> good story as on getting the facts. Sensationalism
> in its various forms was the chief development in
> newspaper content.[19]

These were the days of "yellow journalism," when media moguls like William Randolph Hearst and Joseph Pulitzer were at war with one another over newspaper circulation. No one is sure where the term "yellow journalism" came from in the 1890s, but it was widely understood to describe salacious, over-the-top, scandal-driven journalism that had more interest in attracting readers than in telling the truth.[20] How bad did things get? Bad enough to start a war: "The Spanish-American War would not have occurred had not the appearance of Hearst in New York journalism precipitated a bitter battle for newspaper circulation."[21] To make things worse, this seems not to have been an inadvertent consequence of carelessness, but rather a deliberate effort to boost circulation:

> In the 1890s, plutocrats like William Randolph Hearst and his *Morning Journal* used exaggeration to help spark the Spanish-American War. When Hearst's correspondent in Havana wired that there would be no war, Hearst … famously responded: "You furnish the pictures, I'll furnish the war." Hearst published fake drawings of Cuban officials strip-searching American women—and he got his war.[22]

As bad as this was, Hearst was not the only offender, nor was this the only incident of yellow journalism that led up to the Spanish-American War.

> In 1898, the US Navy battleship, the *USS Maine*, blew up while off Havana, Cuba, killing more than 250 Americans. The cause was never discovered. But the yellow press jumped to the conclusion that the Spanish did it deliberately. "Remember the Maine" became the slogan of the yellow press, driving public opinion toward war.[23]

But then, at the height of the yellow journalism craze, the idea of objectivity began to claw its way forward:

If we look back throughout history, we realize that the rich and powerful have always had an interest (and usually a means) for getting the "little people" to think what they wanted.

In 1896, in the bawdiest days of yellow journalism, the *New York Times* began to climb to its premier position by stressing an "information" model, rather than a "story" model, of reporting. Where the Associated Press was factual to appeal to a politically diverse clientele, the *Times* was informational to attract a relatively select, socially homogeneous readership of the well to do.[24]

With some notable bumps along the way, the notion of objectivity in journalism began to take hold, right up until today, when we seem to be emerging from a period where we have become so spoiled in expecting objectivity from our news sources that we have taken it for granted.

It wasn't until the rise of web-generated news that our era's journalistic notions were seriously challenged, and fake news became a powerful force again. Digital news, you might say, has brought yellow journalism back to the fore.[25]

But let's step back for a moment. From a certain perspective, isn't objectivity and nonpartisanship an amazing thing to expect from a news source? If we look back throughout history, we realize that the rich and powerful have always had an interest (and usually a means) for getting the "little people" to think what they wanted. Before the printed word became an inexpensive source of rival information, one would not be surprised that the king— or whoever controlled the money and politics of the era— really could "create his own reality."[26] This is why the idea of a free media—even one polluted with fake news—was such a revolutionary (and recent) concept. But where did we get the idea that this should come at no cost to us or that we are not required to be active participants in ferreting out the truth? As we have seen, for most of its history the news media has been partisan. Pamphlets were political. Newspapers had owners with business interests and other biases. Indeed, has this ever really changed? Yet we feel entitled to objectivity and are shocked when our news sources do not provide it. But have we been supporting this expectation of fact-based nonpartisan coverage with our dollars? Or really—before the election woke us up—even paid close attention to what was being lost? It is easy to blame technology and claim that "these days it is different." But technology has always had a role in fake news. The printing press and the telegraph each played a part in the ebb and flow of what we expect from journalism. But it has also had an effect on us too. The Internet makes it so easy (and cheap) to get news that we have gotten lazy. Our feeling of entitlement has eroded our critical thinking skills. And isn't this at least part of what has created such a fertile environment for the reemergence of fake news?

Fake News Today

We have had a lot to say so far about the history of fake news, but we still have not defined it. What is fake news? Fake news is not simply news that is false; it is *deliberately* false.[27] It has been created for a purpose. At the beginning of the 2016 election season, perhaps that purpose was "clickbait." They wanted you to click on a provocative headline so that you would add a few cents to their coffers, in much the same way that the *National Enquirer* entices you to slip it into your grocery cart with headlines such as "Hillary: Six Months to Live!" But then the darkness descended. Some of the creators of "fake news" began to notice that the favorable stories about Trump were getting many more clicks than the favorable ones about Hillary—and that the *negative* stories about Hillary were getting the most clicks of all. So guess which ones they doubled down on? In this environment, fake news evolved from clickbait to disinformation. It morphed from a vehicle for financial gain to one for political manipulation.

A good deal of fake news in the 2016 election originated from the Balkans and other parts of Eastern Europe. On November 25, 2016, the *New York Times* ran a story headlined: "Inside a Fake News Sausage Factory: 'This Is All about Income.'"[28] Here we learn about Beqa Latsabidze, a struggling university student from Tbilisi, Georgia, who was living with two roommates and trying to make a little cash off Google ads. He claims that at first he posted positive stories about Hillary Clinton and waited for the cash to roll in, but it didn't work. Then he started to do the same for Donald Trump and found a gold mine. "It's all Trump … people go nuts for it," he said. "My audience likes Trump … I don't want to write bad things about Trump. If I write fake stories about Trump, I lose my audience." So he doubled down on the Hillary-bashing and favorable tales about Trump and made thousands of dollars. His most lucrative story was pure fiction: that the Mexican government had announced they would close their border to Americans if Trump won the White House. When pressed, Latsabidze said that he had no political motive; he was just following the money. He also professed amazement that anyone would mistake anything he had written for real news. "Nobody really believes that Mexico is going to close the border." In fact, he said that he didn't think of what he did as "fake news" at all, but instead saw it as "satire."[29]

Now that all seventeen American intelligence agencies have concluded that the Russian government was actively involved in hacking the US election, such claims of innocence must be taken with a shaker of salt. After the Kremlin broke into the Democratic National Committee's computers in search of information that could be used to manipulate the election—and a good deal of the pro-Trump fake news came from Russia and its satellites—is it really so hard to believe that some of the financial incentive (or at least the idea) behind Hillary-bashing fake news may have come from political sources? The hackers themselves may have been interested only in money, but whose purposes were they serving? Indeed, one tiny town in Macedonia accounted for over a hundred pro-Trump websites. Are we to believe that this was not a coordinated effort and that there was no ideological goal behind it?[30]

This question lingered as the purveyors of fake news jumped the ocean and began to originate from the United States. Two months after the "sausage factory" article, the *New York Times* ran another bombshell about anti-Hillary fake news when it caught up with Cameron Harris, a recent Davidson College graduate and Trump supporter, who was responsible for a "masterpiece" of fake news on his "Christian Times" website. His headline said: "Tens of Thousands of Fraudulent Clinton Votes Found in Ohio Warehouse."[31] Harris invented a janitor, purloined a picture of British ballot boxes from the Internet, and cooked up the whole thing right from his kitchen table. And the story was shared with six million people! Like the Georgian hacker, Harris claimed that his only motive was money. He made about $5,000 in a few days but said that the most important thing was that he learned something. "At first it kind of shocked me," he said, "how easily people would believe it. It was almost like a sociological experiment." When Harris's role in the story came out, he was immediately fired from his job and expressed remorse for what he'd done, though he justified it by saying that fake news had been created on "both sides."[32]

One must of course be careful when speculating about motive. The FBI and congressional investigations of Russian hacking in the 2016 presidential election are still underway and we do not yet know how deeply coordinated these efforts might have been.[33] What does seem clear is that whether or not most of the originators of fake news in the US presidential election had ideological motives, their actions had political impact. How many people who read the story about Hillary's "ballot stuffing" believed it and may have shared it with others who had not yet decided how to vote? Similarly, how many stories in Breitbart and other right-wing outlets that speculated over whether Hillary had a brain tumor amounted at least to "disinformation"—if not outright fake news—intended to have a political effect? Indeed, can't carelessness or willful ignorance serve an ideological goal? After the election, when businessman Eric Tucker tweeted a photo of buses in Austin, Texas, and said that he thought they were being used to bring in paid protestors against Donald Trump, he didn't make a dime, but he certainly had a hand in poisoning the news with his fact-free speculation. His post was shared 16,000 times on Twitter and more than 350,000 times on Facebook, eventually reaching Trump himself, who tweeted that professional protestors were now being incited by the media.[34]

As we saw earlier with the example of science denial, there are those who are lying and those who are lied to, but both are dangerous to the truth. Climate change denial may have started with the economic interests of oil companies, but it quickly became a political ideology with potentially catastrophic impact. Similarly, fake news about the 2016 election may have started as clickbait, but it was soon weaponized as political sabotage. Fake news is a deliberate attempt to get people to react to one's misinformation, whether for the purpose of profit or power. But in either case, the consequences can be dire. Less than a month after the presidential election, a deranged man walked into a Washington, DC, pizzeria and discharged a rifle, saying that he was investigating a story he had read about how Bill and Hillary Clinton were running a child sex slave ring from the business. This was the result of a fake news story (complete with the hashtag #pizzagate) that had been spreading across social media and alt-right websites.[35] Thankfully, no one was hurt. But might there be other potentially harmful consequences of fake news? Buzzfeed reports that in the three months leading up to the 2016 presidential election, the top twenty fake news stories on Facebook got more shares than the top twenty real news stories.[36] Could this have turned the tide for Trump?

If the Spanish-American War was started by fake news, is it so outrageous to think that another war could be too?

Or possibly led to an even more perilous outcome—such as nuclear war?

A few weeks after "pizzagate," the Pakistani defense minister threatened nuclear retaliation against Israel as a result of a fake news story he had read that said "Israeli Defense Minister: If Pakistan sends ground troops to Syria on any pretext, we will destroy their country with a nuclear attack."[37] If the Spanish-American War was started by fake news, is it so outrageous to think that another war could be too? Where might this stop? Fake news is everywhere. If you don't believe me go to Google and type in "did the Holocaust happen?" In December 2016, the top search result would have brought up a neo-Nazi website.[38] The day after the election, the top Google story for "final election result" was a fake story with phony numbers that asserted Trump had won the popular vote.[39]

Down the Rabbit Hole

Throughout his first year as president, Trump has tried to exploit the idea of fake news for his own purposes by branding anything he does not want to believe as fake.[40] From the podium at a pre-inauguration news conference in January 2017, Trump refused to take a question from a CNN reporter, saying that he was reporting fake news. What was the impetus? It seems that CNN had reported that both Trump and Obama had been briefed on a still-unverified intelligence report that had made some salacious claims about Trump. CNN did not report the content of those claims nor say that they were true. All they had done was accurately report that Trump and Obama had been briefed on them. But this was enough for Trump to dismiss it all as "fake news." In the ensuing months, Trump said it was fake news that the media had reported infighting among his aides at the White House, that his poll numbers were falling, and a host of other double-sourced verified factual claims. What a moment in meta-irony. Can the identification of fake news itself now be considered an exercise in spreading fake news?

Here we must remember: fake news is not merely news that is false (or embarrassing, or inconvenient). If the American media is peddling fake news it would have to be *deliberately* falsifying news content. There would have to be an ideological or other purposeful motive behind it. And without evidence to suggest that there is a conspiracy in the American news media, this just seems laughable. We should circle back here to the idea that fake news is *intentionally* false. It is like lying. It is created for the purpose of getting someone to believe what one is saying, even if one knows that it is not true. In this way, one might think that fake news is actually just another word for "propaganda."

In his book *How Propaganda Works*, Jason Stanley disputes this view and makes the point that propaganda should not be confused with biased or even manipulative communication. Propaganda is not necessarily an attempt to convince someone of something that is untrue, nor should one think that all propagandistic claims are made insincerely. Instead, Stanley defines propaganda as a means to exploit and strengthen a flawed ideology.[41] If this is right, it means that any analogy between fake news and propaganda is far more complicated—and dangerous—than what we have so far imagined. For according to Stanley, the purpose of propaganda is not merely to deceive; it is instead an attempt to rule.

In a recent radio interview on NPR, Stanley made the point that the goal of propaganda is to build allegiance.[42] The point is not to communicate information but to get us to "pick a team."[43] To the extent that Trump is using some of the classic techniques of propaganda (stirring up emotions, denigrating critics, scapegoating, seeking division, and fabricating), Stanley warns that we may be headed down the path of authoritarian politics. The goal of propaganda is not to convince someone that you are right, but to demonstrate that you have authority over the truth itself. When a political leader is really powerful, he or she can defy reality. This may sound incredible, but it is not the first time we have heard echoes of this even within American politics. Remember when Karl Rove dismissed critics of the George W. Bush administration as part of the "reality-based community"? Rove then followed up with the memorable (and chilling) observation that "we're an empire now, and when we act, we create our own reality."[44]

Some ideas are so frightening that one hopes they could not be true. Yet Stanley makes the point that this sort of authoritarian defiance over reality can actually be quite popular. To lie and get away with it is the first step in political control. Stanley paraphrases Hannah Arendt when he says "what convinces masses are not facts, and not even invented facts, but rather, open defiance." On a similar subject, Arendt once observed that "the ideal subject of totalitarian rule is not the convinced Nazi or the convinced communist, but people for whom the distinction between fact and fiction ... true and false ... no longer exist."[45]

This takes things pretty far. But even if one disagrees with Stanley, and sees fake news only as intentional deception for some monetary reward (which perhaps had an unfortunate political influence) we would be foolish to ignore the historical parallels, which suggest that such control of information can be a serious political threat. Joseph Goebbels, Hitler's propaganda minister, was a master at exploiting cognitive biases like "source amnesia" and the "repetition effect." Goebbels said that "propaganda works best when those who are being manipulated are confident they are acting on their own free will."[46] Deception, manipulation, and exploitation are recognized tools to create an authoritarian political order.

Trump's strategy is perhaps different from this, yet not unrecognizable:

1. Raise questions about some outlandish matter ("people are talking," "I'm just repeating what I read in the newspaper"), for instance that Obama was not born in the United States or that Obama had Trump wiretapped.

2. Provide no evidence (because there isn't any) beyond one's own conviction.

3. Suggest that the press cannot be trusted because they are biased.

4. This will lead some people to doubt whether what they are hearing from the press is accurate (or at least to conclude that the issue is "controversial").

5. In the face of such uncertainty, people will be more prone to hunker down in their ideology and indulge in confirmation bias by choosing to believe only what fits with their preconceived notions.

6. This is a ripe environment for the proliferation of fake news, which will reinforce items 1 through 5.

7. Thus, people will believe what you say just because you said it. Belief can be tribal. It doesn't take much to get people to believe what they want to believe, if it is being said by someone whom they see as an ally and they are not

being challenged by reliable counterevidence (and sometimes even when they are).

Who needs censorship when the truth can be buried under a pile of bullshit? And isn't this precisely what the issue of post-truth is all about: That truth does not matter as much as feelings? That we can't even tell anymore what is true and what is not?

Timothy Snyder is a Holocaust historian who has written a provocative book called *On Tyranny*.[47] He offers it as a warning to remain aware of the path we're on, where something like fake news and alternative facts can easily march us down the road to authoritarian politics. Indeed, in a recent radio interview, Snyder warned that "post-truth is pre-fascism."[48] This may seem a heavy conclusion to draw from something as facile as fake news. But with today's social media to facilitate the spread of misinformation faster than a propagandist's dream, shouldn't we at least be awake to this possibility?

The question lingers of whether fake news is just propaganda. If fake news is created just to get money from you, it seems more like fraud. But even if it is intended to mislead you into believing a falsehood, one might argue that this is not yet full-blown propaganda. As Stanley argues, the goal of propaganda is not to fool you, but to assert political dominance. Deception can be an effective means of doing this, but it is not the only way. True authoritarians do not need your consent. If post-truth really is pre-fascism, maybe fake news is merely an early tactic, whose purpose is to soften us up for what comes later. Fake news confuses us and makes us doubt whether any source can be trusted. Once we don't know what to believe anymore, this can be exploited. Perhaps true propaganda comes later—once it doesn't matter whether we believe it—because we already know who is in charge.

Fighting Back

We've all seen the charts that purport to show which media outlets are biased and which are reliable.[49] But you know what's coming next don't you? In response, conservative talk show host Alex Jones's website Infowars attacked one popular version and posted his own chart. In just the same way that there are "fact-checker" websites like Snopes, *PolitiFact*, FactCheck, and the *Washington Post*, there are those who claim that these are biased. Indeed there are now even allegations of left-leaning versions of fake news.[50]

What can we do? First, remember that it serves the interest of those who are engaging in deception to succumb to the idea of false equivalence. When we say "a pox on all your houses" we are playing right into the hands of those who would have us believe that there is no such thing as truth. With that principle firmly in mind, here are some concrete steps we can take.

First, recognize the systemic problem and see how it is being exploited. Facebook and Google now account for 85 percent of all new online ad revenue in the United States.[51] They are behemoths. Given that, some have said that they should be the ones to stamp out fake news. Since the election, both Facebook and Google have announced measures to crack down on fake news. Just after the election, Google said that it would ban websites that spread fake news from using its online advertising service.[52] This goes to the heart of all those Balkan and other fake news factories that make money from Google ads one click at a time. But there is a problem: how to be sure that one has identified all and only those websites that promote fake news—and how to handle any backlash? At Facebook, they announced that they would no longer permit ads from websites that displayed misleading or illegal content.[53] Yet here again there is a problem because, according to one computer science expert, "you never really see sponsored posts from fake news sites on Facebook."[54] Most of the fake news that people get from Facebook comes from posts by friends, and it is unclear whether Facebook can (or wants to) do anything about that. Once before they got burned for "interfering" with their trending news feature by using trained editors to vet it rather than an algorithm, and they pulled back after complaints from conservatives.[55] Others have suggested that the giant tech companies should figure out some way to quash fake news with a system of ratings and warnings, just as Facebook now polices its site for nudity and terrorist beheadings, and Google attempts to scrub for child porn. But these attempts to "filter out" fake news along with other objectionable content would surely suffer from accusations that the screeners are being biased in their judgment of biased content.[56]

Are there better methods? According to Brooke Binkowski, managing editor of the fact-checking website Snopes, "pinching off fake news isn't the answer. The answer is flooding it with actual news. And that way, people will continue looking for information, and they will find vetted, nuanced, contextual, in-depth information."[57] While this sounds sensible, it surely will not rehabilitate the most motivated partisans, who look for stories that confirm their preexisting beliefs. Yet it does have the benefit of precedent. After all, isn't "flooding" how fake news became so prominent in the first place? So perhaps the solution is to support investigative news organizations in their mission to provide sourced, vetted, evidence-based coverage. Maybe we should buy those subscriptions to the *New York Times* and the *Washington Post* after all, instead of relying on ten free articles a month. Indeed, as previously noted, some people must already be doing this, for subscriptions are way up at these newspapers and the *Washington Post* has just hired a flood of new journalists.[58]

Second, one might make a bid for more critical thinking. One hopes that colleges and universities are already engaged in this mission. There is a wonderful book by Daniel J. Levitin entitled *Weaponized Lies: How to Think Critically in the Post-Truth Era* (previously published under the title *A Field Guide to Lies*, but retitled after the post-truth craze).[59] Here one can learn all about the techniques of statistics, logic, and good inference that are invaluable to good reasoning.

What about those "digital natives" who are still too young for college, but will grow up in a world of fake news and deception that they must learn to navigate? One of the most heartening stories I've read comes from Scott Bedley, a fifth-grade teacher in Irvine, California, who is teaching his class how to spot fake news by giving them a rubric of things to watch for, then testing them with examples.

> I needed my students to understand that "fake news" is news that is being reported as accurate, but lacks reliability and credibility. A good example are the widely shared stories of the pope endorsing one presidential candidate over another. I decided to devise a game, the goal being to tell fake news from real news. … My students absolutely loved the game. Some refused to go to recess until I gave them another chance to figure out the next article I had queued.[60]

What are the tricks he taught? Actually they are no tricks at all. A fifth-grader can do it. So what excuse do the rest of us have?

1. Look for copyright.

2. Verify from multiple sources.

3. Assess the credibility of the source (e.g., how long has it been around?).

4. Look for a publication date.

5. Assess the author's expertise with the subject.

6. Ask: does this match my prior knowledge?

7. Ask: does this seem realistic?

The only problem with Bedley's system? Now his fifth-graders won't stop fact checking *him*.

Implications for Post-Truth

The problem of fake news is intimately related to the phenomenon of post-truth. Indeed, for many they are one and the same. But this is not quite right, for it is like saying that the existence of nuclear weapons automatically presumes the apocalypse. Just because a weapon exists does not mean that we must be foolish enough to use it. It is how we respond to the challenges that are created by our technology that makes the difference. Social media has played an important role in facilitating post-truth, but again this is a tool rather an outcome. It is a tired cliché to say that "a lie gets halfway around the world before the truth can get its pants on." But that is a fact about untutored human nature, not our potential to rise above it. The electronic dissemination of information can be used to spread lies, but it can also be used to spread truth. If we have ideals worth fighting for, let's fight for them. If our tools are being used as weapons, let's take them back.

DID POSTMODERNISM LEAD TO POST-TRUTH?

So much of left-wing thought is a kind of playing with fire by people who don't even know that fire is hot.

—George Orwell

Some have proposed that the solution to post-truth is to turn to academics, who have for years been thinking about standards of evidence, critical thinking, skepticism, cognitive bias, and so on. It is therefore embarrassing to admit that one of the saddest roots of the post-truth phenomenon seems to have come directly out of colleges and universities.

The concept of postmodernism has been around for more than a century, and has been applied to art, architecture, music, literature, and a host of other creative endeavors. This breadth and longevity, however, does not make it easier to define. According to philosopher Michael

Lynch, "pretty much everyone admits that it is impossible to define postmodernism. This is not surprising, since the word's popularity is largely a function of its obscurity."[1] In what follows, I will do my best.

When one speaks of postmodernism over the last thirty years one is probably talking about a movement that grew out of literary criticism in many colleges and universities in the 1980s, as a result of Jean-François Lyotard's influential 1979 book *The Postmodern Condition: A Report on Knowledge.* There is a rich history of postmodernist thought by many other thinkers from the twentieth century—including Martin Heidegger, Michel Foucault, and Jacques Derrida—that is important as well, but I will have a chance here only to sketch out a few foundational ideas. One was Derrida's theory of "deconstructing" literature, whereby we cannot rely on the idea that an author knew what he or she "meant" in a text so we must break it apart and examine it as a function of the political, social, historical, and cultural assumptions behind it. This was all the rage in humanities departments at colleges and universities throughout North America and Europe during the 1980s and 1990s, as it gave fresh life to the idea that literary scholars could question almost everything they knew about great works of literature.

This idea was soon embraced by sociologists and others who got caught up in the idea that it should apply not just to literary texts but far more broadly, since, in a sense, *everything* could be interpreted as a "text." War, religion, economic relations, sexuality—indeed virtually all of human behavior was freighted with meanings that may or may not be understood by the actors who were engaging in them. Suddenly, the idea that there was a right or wrong answer to what a text (whether written or behavioral) "meant" was thrown into question. Indeed the notion of truth itself was now under scrutiny, for one had to recognize that in the act of deconstruction, the critic was bringing his or her own values, history, and assumptions to the interpretation as well. This meant that there could be *many* answers, rather than just one, for any deconstruction. The postmodernist approach is one in which everything is questioned and little is taken at face value. There is no right answer, only narrative.

Commenting on the philosophical thought of Friedrich Nietzsche (who wrote one hundred years before postmodernism, as one of its precursors), Alexis Papazoglou describes this sort of radical skepticism about the notion of truth in the following way:

> Once we realise that the idea of an absolute, objective truth is a philosophical hoax, the only alternative is a position called "perspectivism"—the idea there is no one objective way the world is, only perspectives on what the world is like.[2]

Think of this as the first thesis of postmodernism: there is no such thing as objective truth. If this is right, though, then how should we react when someone tells us that something is true?

Here we arrive at the second thesis of postmodernism: that any profession of truth is nothing more than a reflection of the political ideology of the person who is making it. Michel Foucault's idea was that our societal life is defined by language, but language itself is shot through with the relations of power and dominance.[3] This means that at base all knowledge claims are really just an assertion of authority; they are a bullying tactic used by the powerful to force those who are weaker to accept their ideological views. Since there is no such thing as "truth," anyone who claims to "know" something is really just trying to oppress us, not educate us. Having power allows us to control what is true, not the other way around. If there are many perspectives, then insisting that we accept any particular one is a form of fascism.

Some will complain that the account just given is not sufficiently detailed or nuanced to do postmodernism justice. Others may object to my thesis that postmodernist thought is in any way a precursor to post-truth. I am confident that further study of postmodernist texts would help to undercut the claim that its ideas may legitimately support right-wing ideology. But I am equally sure that postmodernists have contributed to this situation by retreating within the subtlety of their ideas, then being shocked when they are used for purposes outside what they would approve.

It is true that the right-wing folks who borrow from postmodernist thought do not seem very interested in its nuance. If they need a tool, they will use a boning knife as a hammer. Indeed, thirty years ago conservatives were similarly uninterested in the subtleties of postmodernist thought when they were attacking it as a sign of degeneracy on the left! One might pause here to consider the irony that in just a few decades the right has evolved from critiquing postmodernism—for example, in Lynne Cheney's *Telling the Truth*—to the current situation.[4] This is not to say that postmodernists are completely at fault for how their ideas have been misused, even while they must accept some responsibility for undermining the idea that facts matter in the assessment of reality, and not foreseeing the damage this could cause.

Legitimate questions can of course be raised about the concepts of truth and objectivity—indeed the history of philosophy is very much about those debates—but the complete rejection of and disrespect for truth and objectivity goes too far.[5] If the postmodernists had been content merely to interpret literary texts or even the symbols behind our cultural behavior, things might have been fine. But they weren't. Next they came after natural science.

The Science Wars

As one might expect, there was a big clash when physicists, chemists, biologists, and their fellow scientists (who took themselves to be searching for the truth about reality by testing their theories against empirical evidence) came up against the "social constructivists" (who claimed that all of reality—including scientific theories about it—were socially created and that there was no such thing as objective truth). The "strong programme" of the sociology of science was not precisely the same as what people were doing in literary criticism and cultural studies over in the English Department, but they shared the idea that truth was perspectival and that all knowledge was socially constructed. In this way, the social constructivist movement was kin to postmodernism, and aimed to do for science what their counterparts had done to literature: namely, undermine the claim that there was a single privileged perspective.

The larger field of sociology of science—from which the idea of the social construction of science came—is based on an interesting idea: if scientists said that they were studying nature, who was studying them? If scientists were claiming that their theories were "true," hadn't one better see how these theories were created as scientists worked in their labs? Overnight the field of "science studies" was born. The idea of the strong programme of the sociology of science took things one step further. The "weak" hypothesis was that failed theories must be due to some sort of misfire in the scientific process, perhaps due to ideological bias, that prevented scientists from relying strictly on the evidence. The strong programme said that *all* theories—whether true or false—should be thought of as the product of ideology. If one does not believe that there is such a thing as truth, then it is an open question why scientists favor certain theories over others; to say that it is because of evidence just won't do.[6]

Some claimed that science was really about the personal aggrandizement of scientists who were claiming to be experts on empirical matters. Rather than discovering the truth about nature, they were merely advancing their own agenda of power and exploitation based on their political beliefs.[7] Others pointed out that the language of scientific inquiry was irredeemably sexist and revealed its exploitative nature. It was "prying the secrets loose" from mother nature, forcing her to submit to their examination.[8] One scholar went so far as to claim that Newton's *Principia Mathematica* was a "rape manual."[9]

Then the scientists fought back.

In 1994, Paul Gross (a biologist) and Norman Levitt (a mathematician) published a book called *Higher Superstition: The Academic Left and Its Quarrels with Science*. It was a polemic and a call to arms. They claimed that postmodernism was nonsense and that it was being practiced by people from the humanities who knew next to nothing about how science really worked. Worse, these critics were missing the point of what science was really about: engaging facts rather than values. In any war, it is seldom the case that both sides behave perfectly virtuously. The lack of philosophical nuance in Gross and Levitt's thesis saddens me, as I think they sometimes ignore some of the legitimate criticisms of science.[10] Nonetheless, in war one goes from battle to battle, worrying about the "collateral damage" later. And the next battle was a doozy.

The Sokal Hoax

Sometimes the most effective form of criticism is parody. Inspired by the *Higher Superstition* volume, in 1996 physicist Alan Sokal published a cotton-candy mélange of fawning postmodernism clichés and eyebrow-raising bullshit about quantum mechanics entitled "Transgressing the Boundaries: Towards a Transformative Hermeneutics of Quantum Gravity." And he didn't publish it just anywhere. He sent it to *Social Text*, one of the leading postmodernism journals. How did it happen that they accepted it? Sokal's idea was that if what he had read in Gross and Levitt's book was true, he could get a nonsense paper published if it "(a) sounded good and (b) flattered the editors' ideological preconceptions." And it worked. *Social Text* did not at that time practice "peer review," so the editors never sent the paper out to another scientist who would have caught the puffery. They published it in their next volume, which was, ironically, devoted to "The Science Wars."[11]

Sokal describes his paper as

> a pastiche [of] Derrida and general relativity, Lacan and topology, Irigaray and quantum gravity—held together by vague references to "nonlinearity," "flux," and "interconnectedness." Finally, I jump (again without argument) to the assertion that "post modern science" has abolished the concept of objective reality. Nowhere in all of this is there anything resembling a logical sequence of thought; one finds only citations of authority, plays on words, strained analogies, and bald assertions.[12]

Sokal goes on to point out (as if the point could be missed) the utter absurdity of what he had concocted.

> In the second paragraph I declare, without the slightest evidence or argument, that "physical 'reality' … is at bottom a social and linguistic construct." Not our *theories* of physical reality, mind you, but the reality itself. Fair enough: Anyone who believes that the laws of physics are mere social conventions is invited to try transgressing those

conventions from the windows of my apartment. (I live on the twenty-first floor.)[13]

He goes on to say that although his method was satirical, his motivation was serious. Sokal was angered not merely by the sort of "playing with ideas" that Gross and Levitt had noted in their book, but that this sort of thing was politically irresponsible because it was giving liberalism a bad name.[14] He pointed out that traditionally through the centuries, liberals had been on the side of science and reason, and against mystification and obscurantism. Today, however, he felt that academic humanists were undermining their own political efforts to make the world a better place for the poor and disenfranchised by attacking the roots of evidence-based thought.

> Theorizing about "the social construction of reality" won't help us to find an effective treatment for AIDS or devise strategies for preventing global warming. Nor can we combat false ideas in history, sociology, economics, and politics if we reject the notions of truth and falsity.[15]

Once Sokal's hoax was revealed, the fallout was enormous. There were accusations of bad faith by the editors of *Social Text*, but the sting was undeniable. Many took this as evidence that postmodernist thought was unserious and intellectually bankrupt. And the scientists went back to their labs.

But then a funny thing happened, because once an idea is out there you can't take it back. Although it was an embarrassing moment for postmodernism, it also gave wide publicity to their views and made them available to others who might not have seen them otherwise. And some of those voyeurs were on the right.

Right-Wing Postmodernists

The entire "science wars" debacle led to a question: can postmodernism be used by *anyone* who wants to attack science? Do the techniques work only for liberals (who surely constitute the majority of faculty in literary criticism and cultural studies departments throughout the world), or can they work for others also? Some answer the question by claiming that this is precisely what happened next, as right-wing ideologues, who had a beef against certain scientific claims (like evolution), found within postmodernism the techniques they needed to undermine the idea that scientific theories were superior. This leads naturally to the further question of whether there is today such a thing as "right-wing postmodernism" that uses doubts about truth, objectivity, and power to assert that *all* truth claims are politicized. It would of course be ironic if techniques invented by the left were co-opted by the right in attacking not only science but any sort of evidence-based reasoning. But if this is true, it would go a long way toward establishing another of the root causes of post-truth.

The claim that postmodernism aided and abetted right-wing science denial was made in 2011 by Judith Warner in her article "Fact-Free Science."[16] Here Warner said that "questioning accepted fact, revealing the myths and politics behind established certainties, is a tactic straight out of the left-wing playbook." But, as questioning the science behind global warming "is now a required practice for Republicans eager to play to an emboldened conservative base ... [the] political zeitgeist [has] shifted." She concludes that "attacking science became a sport of the radical right." Where is the evidence that they used postmodernism? Warner includes a few eyebrow-raising quotations from some of the postmodernists themselves, who seem worried over the idea that they have given political cover to conservatives.

This was not enough for science writer Chris Mooney, who seemed irritated by the idea that left-wing postmodernism could be used to undergird right-wing denial. Mooney writes that Warner's analysis is "so wrong that one barely knows how to begin":

First, the idea that conservatives would be strongly influenced by the abstruse arguments and wordplay of left wing academia doesn't make any sense. Do we not recall that starting in the 1970s, conservatives created an armada of ideological think tanks—including many think tanks that now dispute climate change—precisely so as to create their own echo chamber of "expertise" outside of academia? To them, 1990s postmodernism would be the quintessential example of effete academic uselessness. But that's not even the biggest objection to Warner's line of thinking. The biggest objection is that climate change deniers do not look, behave, or sound postmodern in any meaningful sense of the term.[17]

Next he speculates—without much evidence—that most science deniers actually believe in truth, and then he resorts to ridicule:

> The idea that science is the embodiment of "truth" is something with which climate deniers *blithely agree*. They think that they are right and that the scientific consensus about global warming is wrong—objectively. They're not out there questioning whether science is the best way of getting at the truth; they're out there talking as *though their scientists know the truth*. Can you picture [US Senator] James Inhofe citing Derrida or Foucault? The very idea is comical.[18]

I can't help but react to such pronouncements by thinking that they are "so five years ago." Things have changed since 2011, but I think there is also evidence that Warner was right even then and Mooney just missed it.

As we saw in our earlier exploration of science denial in chapter 2, the idea that Trump's minions or his supporters would have to be reading postmodernist literature in order to be influenced by it flies in the face of how doubt is "manufactured." Mooney is correct that a good deal of the initial work is done in ideological think tanks. By the time it gets to government officials and lobbyists it is only a series of talking points. But it is also important to realize that the tactics invented in one battle of science denial are often appropriated for the next. We have already seen from Oreskes and Conway that the "tobacco strategy" was successfully employed long after the skirmish over cigarettes and cancer was "won" by fighting it to a stalemate. The idea of "fighting the science" and claiming that "the truth is uncertain" was also used in the fight over acid rain, the ozone hole, and many others to follow. And one needs to remember the historical sequence too. For what was the battle immediately before climate change, from which the global warming skeptics got a lot of their weaponry? Evolution.

There is little doubt that postmodernist thought had an important influence on this debate, as Creationism morphed into "Intelligent Design" (ID) and began a series of battles to "teach the controversy" over ID theory versus evolution within public school biology classrooms. How do we know? Because one of the founders of ID theory—Phillip Johnson, who helped to create one of the think tanks that Mooney refers to—said that it did.

In a pathbreaking scholarly article, philosopher of science Robert Pennock convincingly argues that "the deep threads of post-modernism … run through the ID Creationist movement's arguments, as evidenced in the writings and interviews of its key leaders."[19] Indeed, he makes the provocative claim that "Intelligent Design Creationism is the bastard child of Christian fundamentalism and post-modernism." He does so by documenting the statements of Johnson, "the godfather of the ID movement."

Pennock tells a fascinating story about the founding of the Discovery Institute in Seattle, Washington, and its debt to "deep-pocket right-wing political backers." He claims that to this day "the Discovery Institute is still flogging the postmodern horse." When did this horse get created? He claims that this was due almost single-handedly to the influence of Johnson. It is not a subtle matter to see the influence of postmodernism in Johnson's work. He embraces it explicitly. By examining not only Johnson's published writings but also his interviews, Pennock has found statements that seem incontrovertible:

> The great problem from the Christian viewpoint
> is that the whole controversy over evolution has

traditionally been phrased as a Bible vs. Science issue, and then the question becomes how do you defend the Bible? ... Now, the problem with approaching it this way is that in our culture it is understood that science is some objective fact-finding proceeding. And if you are arguing the Bible vs. Science, then people think that you are arguing for blind faith against objectively determined knowledge or experiment.[20]

My plan, as it were, is to deconstruct those philosophical barriers ... I'm relativizing the philosophical system.[21]

I told them I was a postmodernist and deconstructionist just like them, but aiming at a slightly different target.[22]

In another interview, Johnson self-consciously appeals to the "strong programme" of the sociology of scientific knowledge, which, as Pennock points out, "is not the same as, but does have close conceptual affinities to postmodernism." Johnson makes clear not only that he has read this literature, but that he wants to use it to defend ID theory against the "objective" claims of evolutionary science. He states that "the curious thing is that the sociology-of-knowledge approach has not yet been applied to Darwinism. That is basically what I do in my manuscript."[23]

Pennock's article contains numerous other references to occasions when Johnson reveals his desire to use the postmodernist approach to undercut the professed epistemic authority of evolution by natural selection, and use it to defend ID theory as an alternative. Pennock explains the point of this strategy:

Do not think that science has anything to do with reality; evolution is just an imaginative story. It just happens to be one told by the science tribe. On the radical postmodern view, science has no special privilege over any other views of the world even with regard to matters of empirical fact; every tribe may take its own story as the starting point for its other beliefs. ID creationists are equally justified in taking God's creation and will for man as their starting assumption.[24]

It could not be clearer that postmodernist thought had an influence on ID theory. It is also not in doubt that ID theory provided the blueprint for how climate change deniers would later fight their own battles: attack the existing science, identify and fund your own experts, push the idea that the issue is "controversial," get your own side out through the media and lobbying, and watch the public react.[25] Even

Even if right-wing politicians and other science deniers were not reading Derrida and Foucault, the germ of the idea made its way to them.

if right-wing politicians and other science deniers were not reading Derrida and Foucault, the germ of the idea made its way to them: science does not have a monopoly on the truth. It is therefore not unreasonable to think that right-wingers are using some of the same arguments and techniques of postmodernism to attack the truth of other scientific claims that clash with their conservative ideology.

Is there any evidence of this? Here we should turn to some of the "mea culpas" from postmodernists themselves, who have been horrified to see how some of their ideas have been used for right-wing purposes.[26] Bruno Latour, one of the founders of social constructivism, wrote in a 2004 piece "Why Has Critique Run Out of Steam?" that he became concerned when he saw an editorial in the *New York Times* that said:

> Most scientists believe that [global] warming is caused largely by manmade pollutants that require strict regulation. Mr. Luntz [a Republican strategist] seems to acknowledge as much when he says that "the scientific debate is closing against us." His advice, however, is to emphasize that the evidence is not complete. "Should the public come to believe that the scientific issues are settled," he writes, "their views about global warming will change accordingly. Therefore, you need to continue to make the lack of scientific certainty a primary issue."[27]

Latour's reaction to this is not unlike that of an arms dealer who learns that one of his weapons has been used to kill an innocent:

> Do you see why I am worried? I myself have spent some time in the past trying to show "the lack of scientific certainty" inherent in the construction of facts. I too made it a "primary issue." But I did not exactly aim at fooling the public by obscuring the certainty of a closed argument—or did I? After all, I have been accused of just that sin. Still, I'd like to believe that, on the contrary, I intended to emancipate the public from prematurely naturalized objectified facts. Was I foolishly mistaken? Have things changed so fast?[28]

Worse, the weapons factory is still open.

> Entire Ph.D. programs are still running to make sure that good American kids are learning the hard way that facts are made up, that there is no such thing as natural, unmediated, unbiased access to truth, that we are always prisoners of language, that we always speak from a particular standpoint, and so on, while dangerous extremists are using the very same argument of social construction to destroy hard-won evidence that could save our lives. Was I wrong

to participate in the invention of this field known as science studies? Is it enough to say that we did not really mean what we said? Why does it burn my tongue to say that global warming is a fact whether you like it or not? Why can't I simply say that the argument is closed for good?[29]

One doesn't find a more full-blooded expression of regret in academe than this. And Latour is not the only post-modernist to notice his fingerprints on the strategy of right-wing science denial. Michael Berube, a humanist and literary critic, wrote this in 2011:

Now the climate-change deniers and the young-Earth creationists are coming after the natural scientists, just as I predicted—and they're using some of the very arguments developed by an academic left that thought it was speaking only to people of like mind. Some standard left arguments, combined with the left populist distrust of "experts" and "professionals" and assorted high-and-mighty muckety-mucks who think they're the boss of us, were fashioned by the right into a powerful device for delegitimating scientific research.[30]

Indeed, his shame is so great that by the end of his piece, Berube seems in a mood to bargain:

I'll admit that you were right about the potential for science studies to go horribly wrong and give fuel to deeply ignorant and/or reactionary people. And in return, you'll admit that I was right about the culture wars, and right that the natural sciences would not be held harmless from the right-wing noise machine. And if you'll go further, and acknowledge that some circumspect, well-informed critiques of actually existing science have merit (such as the criticism that the postwar medicalization of pregnancy and childbirth had some ill effects), I'll go further too, and acknowledge that many humanists' critiques of science and reason are neither circumspect nor well-informed. Then perhaps we can get down to the business of how to develop safe, sustainable energy and other social practices that will keep the planet habitable.[31]

This soul searching on the left is completely ignored by those who are afraid that post-truth will now be laid at the feet of postmodernism, yet the pathway from science denial to full-blown reality denial itself seems undeniable. What would an application of postmodernism to post-truth politics look like? It looks a lot like the world we now inhabit:

If there are really no facts and only interpretations, and if millions of Americans are ready to unthinkingly embrace your perspective, then why bother adhering to a rigid line that separates fact from fiction? If you interpret a period of cold weather as evidence that climate change isn't happening, and if millions of other people agree with your point of view, then climate change is a hoax. If your subjective experience perceives record attendance at the inauguration, then there was record attendance— aerial photographs that prove otherwise are simply illustrating another perspective.[32]

One can almost hear Kellyanne Conway defending Sean Spicer's use of "alternative facts."

What a complete misfire of the original politics that motivated postmodernism, which was to protect the poor and vulnerable from being exploited by those in authority. It is now the poor and vulnerable who will suffer most from climate change. Sokal's prediction is close to being fulfilled, for how does the left fight back against right-wing ideology without using facts? This is the cost of playing with ideas as if they had no consequences. It's all fun and games to attack truth in the academy, but what happens when one's tactics leak out into the hands of science deniers and conspiracy theorists, or thin-skinned politicians who insist that their instincts are better than any evidence?[33]

How does the left fight back against right-wing ideology without using facts? This is the cost of playing with ideas as if they had no consequences.

So which is it? Does the left believe in truth or not? There will be split allegiance perhaps for some, who now find themselves in the uncomfortable position of either giving aid and comfort to the enemy or defending the idea that there is such a thing as truth. Yet the question lingers: how can we be sure that postmodernism has made the jump from right-wing science denial to the full-blown, reality-bending brand of skepticism that is post-truth? Since Trump has taken office, this question has come out of the shadows.[34] One finds a handful of articles now in the mainstream media that take the question seriously,[35] but some still seem stuck on the idea that unless one can find Kellyanne Conway reading Derrida, this is all just speculation.[36] Some also claim that it is ridiculous to see postmodernism and post-truth as cause and effect because post-truth has been around much longer than one thinks, and postmodernism is in fact quite useful for giving us a vocabulary to talk about post-truth, even if it is not its cause.[37]

Yet there is one philosopher who seems completely willing to draw a connection. In a February 12, 2017, interview with the *Guardian*, Daniel Dennett places the blame for post-truth squarely at the feet of postmodernism:

> Philosophy has not covered itself in glory in the way it has handled this [questions of fact and truth]. Maybe people will now begin to realise that philosophers aren't quite so innocuous after all.

Sometimes, views can have terrifying consequences that might actually come true. I think what the postmodernists did was truly evil. They are responsible for the intellectual fad that made it respectable to be cynical about truth and facts. You'd have people going around say: "Well, you're part of that crowd who still believe in facts."[38]

Is there more direct evidence than this? Something more like what Roger Pennock did to show that postmodernism was at the root of ID theory? As a matter of fact, there is.

Trolling for Trump

One cannot understand the rise of post-truth (or Trump) without acknowledging the importance of the alternative media. Without Breitbart, Infowars, and all of the other alt-right media outlets, Trump likely would not have been able to get his word out to the people who were most disposed to believe his message. The important point here—as we saw in chapter 5—is that the news is now fragmented. People are not confined to learning the "truth" from just one or a few sources anymore. And in fact they are not limited to getting it only from "the media" either. A good deal of Trump's support during the election came from alt-right bloggers. One of the most influential was Mike Cernovich.

Mike Cernovich is a pro-Trump, "American nationalist," conspiracy-theory-loving blogger with 250,000 Twitter followers.[39] But he is not just any blogger. He has been profiled in the *New Yorker* and the *Washington Post*, and was interviewed by CBS anchorman Scott Pelley, based on the depth of his influence on the 2016 presidential election. Cernovich is dismissed by some as a regular contributor to the steady stream of "fake news."[40] He is the person who pushed the #HillarysHealth tweets that said she was dying.[41] Remember the #pizzagate story about how Bill and Hillary Clinton were running a child sex slave ring out of a DC pizza restaurant, where someone almost got shot? Cernovich was one of the people who promoted it.[42] He has also accused the Clinton campaign of participating in a satanic sex cult.[43] In his interview with the *New Yorker*, Cernovich talks about some of his other controversial ideas, such as that date rape doesn't really exist and that his first marriage was ruined by "feminist indoctrination."[44]

And he has come to the favorable attention of the Trump administration. In April 2017, Mike Cernovich was congratulated by Donald Trump Jr. in a tweet that said Cernovich should "win the Pulitzer" for breaking the story about Susan Rice's alleged unmasking of intelligence reports related to Trump campaign officials. When Kellyanne Conway learned of Cernovich's upcoming interview with Scott Pelley, she told her Twitter followers to watch the exchange or read the entire transcript, and directed them to Cernovich's site. One of Cernovich's critics has said "I think Conway and Trump Jr attempting to elevate Cernovich says a lot about Trump's White House and how they will resort to conspiracy theorists if it helps to distract from things that hurt them."[45]

Cernovich clearly has great influence. So what about the question of postmodernism? In the *New Yorker* article, one comes across this little nugget:

> Let's say, for the sake of argument, that Walter Cronkite lied about *everything*. Before Twitter, how would you have known? Look, I read postmodernist theory in college. If everything is a narrative, then we need alternatives to the dominant narrative. I don't look like a guy who reads Lacan, do I?[46]

Cernovich may seem like a luddite, but he is actually quite well educated. He has a law degree from Pepperdine and seems to have been paying attention in college. And he makes a familiar point: If there is no truth, and it is all just perspective, how can we ever really know anything? Why not doubt the mainstream news or embrace a conspiracy theory? Indeed, if news is just political expression, why not make it up? Whose facts should be dominant? Whose perspective is the right one?

Thus is postmodernism the godfather of post-truth.

FIGHTING POST-TRUTH

We have now sunk to a depth at which restatement of the
obvious is the first duty of intelligent men.

—George Orwell

On April 3, 2017, *Time* magazine released an issue with a
cover story that asked "Is Truth Dead?" It is a striking piece
of art, reminiscent of another they did in a previous time of
turmoil—the 1960s—that asked the same question about
God. By April 1966, President Kennedy had been assassi-
nated, America's commitment to the Vietnam War had es-
calated sharply, crime back home was rising, and Americans
were at the dawn of an era in which they would begin to
lose faith in their institutions. It was a moment of national
reflection about the path we were heading down. The occa-
sion for *Time*'s most recent announcement of a moment of
national reflection was the Trump presidency itself.

In the opening essay, editor Nancy Gibbs asks some momentous questions about our commitment to the idea of truth "in the face of a President who treats it like a toy." These are strong words, but they are followed by some observations that are even more shocking:

> For Donald Trump, shamelessness is not just a strength, it's a strategy. ... Whether it's the size of his inaugural crowds or voter fraud or NATO funding or the claim that he was wiretapped, Trump says a great many things that are demonstrably false. But indicting Trump as a serial liar risks missing a more disturbing question: What does he actually believe? Does it count as lying if he believes what he says? ... Where is the line between lie, spin and delusion? Or, as his adviser Kellyanne Conway memorably put it, between facts and alternative facts, the conclusions that he wants the audience to reach vs. the conclusions warranted by the evidence at hand?[1]

Noting that 70 percent of Trump's campaign statements were judged by *PolitiFact* to be false, that nearly two-thirds of voters polled during the campaign said that Trump was not trustworthy, *but he won the election anyway*, one cannot help but wonder whether the threat to truth far outstrips the actions of any one man.[2] If so, the question on the cover of *Time* is not just hyperbole but frighteningly pertinent: *Is* truth dead?

Throughout this book we have explored the roots of post-truth, on the assumption that one cannot really do anything about a problem unless one understands what caused it. But now it is time to ask the payoff question: can anything be done about post-truth? In 2008, Farhad Manjoo published a book (that he wrote in 2006) called *True Enough: Learning to Live in a Post-Fact Society*.[3] It is amazing that someone got out so far ahead of the curve to more or less see what was coming at the level of national politics.[4] Manjoo's book was written before the smartphone had been invented. Barack Obama wasn't even a blip on the national radar screen. In fact, one of the salient examples Manjoo explores is the "Swift Boat Veterans for Truth" campaign that was cooked up against John Kerry when he ran against George W. Bush in 2004. Here the manipulation of cognitive bias and presentation of a "counternarrative" for the media on a national stage came into focus. With hindsight, it is easy to connect the dots to what came later in 2016, but Manjoo foresaw the ideas of media fragmentation, information bias, the decline of objectivity, and the threat not just to knowing the truth but to the idea of truth itself.

What does he offer to help us combat it? Unfortunately, not much. Despite a late chapter titled "Living in a World without Trust," Manjoo does not offer much practical advice beyond saying that we should "choose wisely" what we are going to believe. Perhaps it is too much to ask that someone who saw so far ahead would also provide us with the tools to fight what was coming (for if we had listened, maybe it wouldn't have happened). Here I will try to push things further. We don't need to see what is coming anymore; we are living through it. We may now understand a little better why post-truth happened, but how can this help us to contend with it? As Manjoo's subtitle asks: can we learn to live in a post-fact society?

I, for one, do not want to. The issue for me is not to learn how to adjust to living in a world in which facts do not matter, but instead to stand up for the notion of truth and learn how to fight back. Indeed, here is the first bit of practical advice we should come to terms with, which John Kerry brutally learned during the "Swift Boat Veterans for Truth" campaign, when a few right-wing veterans were spinning tales intended to undermine Kerry's stellar war record. Only one of the Swift Boat Veterans, George Elliot, had actually served with Kerry in Vietnam, and he publicly recanted his story of Kerry's alleged war-time cowardice soon after the first Swift Boat ads started to appear on TV. But by then it was too late. Money was pouring in from Texas millionaires and others who were sympathetic to the cause. Elliot's recantation was dismissed because of a fake news story that said that the *Boston Globe* reporter who had broken the story of Elliot's recantation had been commissioned to write the foreword to the Kerry–Edwards campaign book. That was a lie, but it hardly mattered. The tribes had chosen their sides. But then Kerry made a fatal error by choosing not to "dignify" the Swift Boat Veterans' claims with a response for two solid weeks while they pummeled him on national TV. He lost the election by a few thousand votes in Ohio. Kerry had no idea we were entering the post-truth era.[5]

The lesson here is that one must always fight back against lies. We should never assume that any claim is "too outrageous to be believed." A lie is told because the person telling it thinks there is a chance that someone will believe it. We might hope that the listener has enough common sense not to believe it, but in an age of partisan manipulation and fragmentation of our information sources, keyed to play on our motivated reasoning, we are no longer entitled to that assumption. The point of challenging a lie is not to convince the liar, who is likely too far gone in his or her dark purpose to be rehabilitated. But because every lie has an audience, there may still be time to do some good for others. If we do not confront a liar, will those who have not yet moved from ignorance to "willful ignorance" just slip further down the rabbit hole toward full-blown denialism, where they may not even listen to facts or reason anymore? Without a "counternarrative" from us, will they have any reason to doubt what the liar is saying? At the very least it is important to *witness* a lie and call it out for

In an era of post-truth, we must challenge each and every attempt to obfuscate a factual matter and challenge falsehoods before they are allowed to fester.

what it is. In an era of post-truth, we must challenge each and every attempt to obfuscate a factual matter and challenge falsehoods before they are allowed to fester.

Although the voices on the other side may be loud, it is a powerful thing to have the facts. This is to say that even in an era of partisan bloviating and noisy "skepticism," the facts about reality can only be denied for so long. The media stopped telling "both sides of the story" about vaccines and autism once there was a measles outbreak in fourteen states in 2015. All of a sudden, the facts of Wakefield's fraud made better copy. One could almost see the TV hosts' anxiety over their earlier complicity. Overnight, there were no more split-screen TV debates between experts and skeptics. False equivalence no longer seemed like such a good idea once people started getting hurt.

Can the same thing now happen on other topics, such as climate change? To a certain extent it already has. As of July 2014, the BBC decided to stop giving equal airtime to climate change deniers.[6] The *Huffington Post* made the same decision in April 2012, when its founder Arianna Huffington said:

> In all our stories, especially matters of controversy, we strive to consider the strongest arguments we can find on all sides, seeking to deliver both nuance and clarity. Our goal is not to please those whom we report on or to produce stories that create the

appearance of balance, but to seek the truth. ... If the balance of evidence in a matter of controversy weighs heavily on one side, we acknowledge it in our reports. We strive to give our audience confidence that all sides have been considered and represented fairly.[7]

But what good will this do? If we are truly living in a post-truth era, it is unclear whether any policy change by the media will matter. If our beliefs about something like climate change are already determined by our cognitive biases and political ideology, how would we ever break out of our worldview? For one thing, why wouldn't we just change the channel? Even if we hear the truth, won't we reject it?

As a matter of fact, no. Not always. Although the forces of motivated reasoning, confirmation bias, and some of the other influences we have talked about in this book are strong, remember that empirical evidence suggests that the repetition of true facts does eventually have an effect. Recall here the research of David Redlawsk et al., which we briefly discussed in chapter 3.[8] In the subtitle of their paper, they ask the pertinent question, "do motivated reasoners ever get it?" They acknowledge the work of Nyhan, Reifler, and others who have shown that those in the grips of partisan bias are strongly motivated to reject evidence that is dissonant with their beliefs, sometimes even leading to a "backfire effect." But are there any limits to this? In their paper, Redlawsk et al. observe that:

> It seems unlikely that voters do this ad infinitum. To do so would suggest continued motivated reasoning even in the face of extensive disconfirming information. In this study we consider whether motivated reasoning processes can be overcome simply by continuing to encounter information incongruent with their expectations. If so, voters must reach a tipping point after which they begin more accurately updating their evaluations.[9]

And this is exactly what was found. Redlawsk and colleagues discovered experimental evidence that "an affective tipping point does in fact exist," which suggests that "voters are not immune to disconfirming information after all, even when initially acting as motivated reasoners."[10] James Kuklinski and colleagues learned in another study that although misinformed beliefs can be quite stubborn, it is possible to change partisans' minds when one "hits them between the eyes" over and over with factually correct information.[11] It may not be easy to convince people with inconvenient facts, but it is apparently possible.

And this makes sense, doesn't it? We have all heard examples of people who won the "Darwin Award" by denying reality until they met their demise. It just doesn't compute that evolution would allow us to resist truth forever. Eventually, when it makes a difference to us, we are capable of resolving our cognitive dissonance by rejecting our ideological beliefs rather than the facts. Indeed, there is good evidence that this can occur not just in the lab but in the real world as well.

The city of Coral Gables, Florida, sits at nine feet above sea level. Scientists project that in a few decades it will be under water. Soon after the new mayor James Cason, a Republican, was elected he heard a lecture about climate change and its effect on South Florida. And he was flabbergasted. "You know, I'd read some articles here and there, but I didn't realize how impactful it would be on the city that *I'm* now the leader of."[12] Since then, Cason has tried to raise a warning cry, but he hasn't had much luck:

> Some say, "I don't believe it." Some say, "Well, tell me what I can do about it, and I'll get concerned." Others say, "I've got other things I'm worried about now, and I'll put that off." And others say, "I'll leave that to my grandkids to figure out."[13]

Cason is beginning to look into the question of legal liability. And he's continuing to sound the alarm, hoping that his fellow Republicans at the national level will begin to take global warming seriously before it's too late. On the eve of one of the 2016 Republican debates, Cason published an op-ed in the *Miami Herald*, along with his Republican counterpart Mayor Tomas Regaldo of Miami. They wrote:

> As staunch Republicans, we share our party's suspicion of government overreach and unreasonable regulations. But for us and most other public officials in South Florida, climate change is not a partisan talking point. It's a looming crisis that we must deal with—and soon.[14]

If the word "schadenfreude" did not already exist, it is at this point that progressives probably would have had to invent it ... except for the fact that we are all in the same boat—or soon will be—and cannot afford to indulge in the feeling of self-righteousness. Even if you are prepared to deny the facts, they have a way of asserting themselves. When the water creeps up on their $5 million houses or their businesses are affected, people will eventually listen. But does this mean that in the meantime we just have to wait? No. One can support critical thinking and investigative reporting. One can call out liars. Even before the water rises, we should try to figure out some way to "hit people between the eyes" with facts.

This strategy, however, should be implemented carefully. Psychological research has also shown that when people feel insecure and threatened they are less likely to listen. In a recent study by Brendan Nyhan and Jason Reifler, subjects were given a self-affirmation exercise, then exposed to new information. It was hypothesized that people who felt better about themselves might be more open to accepting information that corrected their misperceptions. The researchers found a weak correlation, but it was not consistent; it worked on some topics but not others. Another finding from the same study was more robust: information provided in graphical form was more convincing than narratives.[15] So what should we take away from this? That it is probably helpful not to yell at a misinformed person whom you are trying to convince, but the best thing of all is to silently give him or her a graph?

It is hard to try to depoliticize factual questions, especially when we feel that the "other side" is being ridiculous or stubborn. It is probably helpful to realize that the same tendencies exist within us too. And there is a lesson here, which is that one of the most important ways to fight back against post-truth is to fight it within ourselves. Whether we are liberals or conservatives, we are all prone to the sorts of cognitive biases that can lead to post-truth. One should not assume that post-truth arises only from others, or that its results are somebody else's problem. It is easy to identify a truth that someone else does not want to see. But how many of us are prepared to do this with our *own* beliefs? To doubt something that *we want to believe*, even though a little piece of us whispers that we do not have all the facts?

One of the barriers to critical thinking is bathing in a constant stream of confirmation bias. If you are getting your information primarily from one source—or you find yourself responding emotionally to what you are hearing from one particular channel—it is probably time to diversify your news feed. Remember the people in the "2, 4, 6" experiment who never tried to disprove what they thought they "knew"? We must not do that. This is not to say that we should start to consume fake news. Nor does it mean that we are justified in drawing some sort of false equivalence between Fox and CNN. But it does mean that we should learn how to vet news sources properly and ask ourselves how it is that we "know" that something we are hearing is fake. Is it just because it makes us mad or—like those fifth graders in Mr. Bedley's class—do we have a rubric? Especially if we are hearing things that we want to believe, we must learn to be more skeptical. Indeed, this is a lesson taught to us by science.

There is no such thing as liberal science or conservative science. When we are asking an empirical question, what should count most is the evidence. As Senator Daniel Patrick Moynihan said long ago (on another topic): "You are entitled to your own opinion, but not your own facts." The strength of science is that it embraces an attitude of constantly checking one's beliefs against the empirical

Whether we are liberals or conservatives, we are all prone to the sorts of cognitive biases that can lead to post-truth. One should not assume that post-truth arises only from others, or that its results are somebody else's problem.

evidence, and changing those beliefs as one learns what the facts are. Can we vow to bring a little bit of this attitude to our consideration of other factual matters? If not, I'm afraid there is an even greater danger out there than post-truth.

Are We Entering the Pre-Truth Era?

In a recent article in the *Washington Post*, Ruth Marcus was more troubled than usual by Trump's interview with *Time* magazine.[16] In that interview Trump said all sorts of things that drove the fact checkers crazy.[17] He got a cascade of "Pinocchios" from the *Washington Post* and reprimands from the *New York Times* and other news sources for his misstatements (or lies).[18] But Marcus was concerned about something beyond Trump's mendacity.

In this interview, Trump said "I'm a very instinctual person, but my instinct turns out to be right." By this he seemed to have meant that even if some of the things he had said couldn't be borne out by the evidence, they were still true. By this he did *not* seem to mean that the evidence existed, but he was the only one who had seen it. Instead, he seemed to feel that his believing something somehow *made* it true. More than a mere penchant for accurate prediction, Trump spoke as if he had the power to change reality. As Marcus put it: "If an assertion isn't true, no worry.

President Trump will find a way to make it so, or at least claim it is."[19]

For example, at a rally on February 11, 2017, Trump made an obscure reference to "what's happened last night in Sweden." The people of Sweden were puzzled. To their knowledge, nothing had happened the previous night. It turned out that Trump had been referencing a story he saw on Fox News about immigrants in Sweden; nothing had "happened." Then two days later—perhaps as a result of Trump's amplification of the issue—riots broke out in an immigrant neighborhood in Stockholm. In his *Time* interview, Trump took credit for being right:

> Sweden. I make the statement, everyone goes crazy. The next day they have a massive riot, and death, and problems. … A day later they had a horrible, horrible riot in Sweden, and you saw what happened.[20]

Does that mean Trump had been "right"? Of course not. The riot had not been "last night," it was not "massive," and there had been no deaths. But in Trump's mind, it vindicated him.

Consider another example: in the early morning hours of March 4, 2017, Trump tweeted that President Obama had had his "wires tapped" at Trump Tower during the presidential campaign. (Again, Trump was likely reacting to a Fox News story and could produce no evidence.)

Inquiries through the FBI, NSA, FISA, and other credible sources turned up no evidence that this had actually taken place. Then on March 24, Rep. Devin Nunes (Republican chairman of the House Intelligence Committee) held a press conference in which he said that he had just briefed the president on some deeply troubling facts that he had learned from a confidential source, which had something to do with Trump's surveillance. As it turned out, those "facts" had been provided to Nunes the night before by two of Trump's aides. As Congress and the media bore down, it was eventually learned that some of Trump aides had been incidentally surveilled in a routine intelligence-gathering operation of Russian officials. (What Trump's aides had been doing talking to those Russian officials has not yet been determined.) But Trump took this to be vindication of his earlier claim. He said "So that means I'm right" and said that he felt "vindicated." Even though there was no way he could have known about it at the time—and it is an open question whether this sort of incidental collection of phone conversations involving his aides counts as having his "wires tapped"—let alone by President Obama—Trump took credit for it.

What is going on here?

According to Marcus, "it is not simply that Trump refuses to accept reality, it is that he bends it to his will." In another analysis of Trump's *Time* interview from the *Guardian* newspaper, the conclusion is a bit more expansive:

In Trumpspeak, truth is not factual. ... Truthful statements do not necessarily offer an accurate account of events in the world. They provide an approximation or exaggeration of something that might, in theory have occurred. Whether a terror attack in Sweden ever took place on the night named by the president is irrelevant. Nor should we care that the riot was not massive and there was no death. Close and maybe are good enough.

In Trumpspeak, belief is a signal of truth. If his supporters believe him, then what Trump is saying must be true. Conversely, if his detractors disbelieve him, this too is evidence that what he is saying must be true.

Finally, Trumpspeak is transactional. It places no independent value on truth. The value of speech is to be measured exclusively in terms of its effects. If a statement gets me closer to my goal, then it is valuable; if it does not, it is worthless. Valuable statements, then, are true by virtue of the fact that they advance my interests. Statements that fail to do so are worthless and thus false.[21]

One wonders whether this is post-truth or something else. Is this merely a case where "objective facts are less influential in shaping [belief] than appeals to emotion?" Or is this something closer to delusion? When Marcus speaks of "pre-truth," she seems to mean a situation in which Trump believes not only that he can see things before they happen, but that his belief can *make* them happen.[22] This is not based on any evidence that he can share with others, but instead a feeling that he can intuit or even control the future—or the past. Psychologists call this "magical thinking."

Is this something to worry about, or is it merely to be expected from a person who keeps score according to whether a belief, event, or piece of information flatters him? As Trump has repeatedly tweeted, "any negative polls are fake news." Just so. But people do worry about this because it suggests either a deep-seated effort to manipulate people into rejecting reality or a break with reality itself.

I do not flatter myself to think that I can foresee the future. But when we become untethered from truth we become untethered from reality. Just as the water will continue to rise on the homes in Coral Gables, Florida— whether its residents believe it or not—so will the consequences of post-truth creep up on all of us unless we are prepared to fight them. We may be able to bullshit others (or ourselves) for a while and get away with it, but eventually we will pay a price for thinking that we can create our own reality.

On January 28, 1986, the space shuttle *Challenger* broke apart just seventy-three seconds after its launch from Cape Canaveral, Florida, killing its entire crew. The science that had been used to create the shuttle had been rigorous and this was not its first mission. After the disaster, President Reagan appointed a special commission of prominent scientists and astronauts to look into what had gone wrong. While the engineering was sound, upon investigation it was learned that there had been preexisting concerns about the ability of the rubber O-rings on the shuttle to withstand cold temperatures, which would cause them to buckle. The shuttle was not recommended for launch in subfreezing temperatures. January 28 was an unusually cold day in Florida. So why had the shuttle been scheduled for launch? It was an administrative decision, made over the objection of some NASA engineers.

The problem with the O-rings was dramatically illustrated by Nobel-Prize-winning physicist Richard Feynman, a member of the commission, who dunked one of the O-rings in a pitcher of ice water that was sitting on the table at one of the public hearings. The facts were the facts. No amount of spin, lies, bullshit, or happy talk could contradict them. After the shuttle crashed, no one much cared about the instinct or intuition of the NASA officials who had thought they could control reality. Soon after, Feynman released a statement that included the following phrase: "for a successful technology, reality must take precedence over public relations, for nature cannot be fooled."[23]

It is our decision how we will react to a world in which someone is trying to pull the wool over our eyes. Truth still matters, as it always has. Whether we realize this in time is up to us.

Whether we call it post-truth or pre-truth, it is dangerous to ignore reality. And that is what we are talking about here. The danger of post-truth is not just that we allow our opinions and feelings to play a role in shaping what we think of as facts and truth, but that by doing so we take the risk of being estranged from reality itself.

But there is another possible path.

We are not post-truth any more than we are pre-truth, unless we allow ourselves to be. Post-truth is not about reality; it is about the way that humans *react* to reality. Once we are aware of our cognitive biases, we are in a better position to subvert them. If we want better news media outlets, we can support them. If someone lies to us, we can choose whether to believe him or her, and then challenge any falsehoods. It is our decision how we will react to a world in which someone is trying to pull the wool over our eyes. Truth still matters, as it always has. Whether we realize this in time is up to us.

GLOSSARY

Alternative facts
Information that is provided to challenge the narrative created by facts that are hostile to one's preferred beliefs.

Backfire effect
Psychological phenomenon where the presentation of true information that conflicts with someone's mistaken beliefs causes them to hold those beliefs even more strongly.

Cognitive dissonance
Psychological state wherein we simultaneously believe two things that are in conflict with one another, which creates psychic tension.

Confirmation bias
Tendency to give more weight to information that confirms one of our pre-existing beliefs.

Dunning–Kruger effect
Psychological phenomenon wherein our lack of ability causes us to vastly over-estimate our actual skill.

Fake news
Disinformation that is deliberately created to look like actual news in order to have a political effect.

False equivalence
To suggest that there is equal value between two points of view, when it is obvious that one is much closer to the truth. Often used to avoid accusations of partisan bias.

Information silo
Tendency to seek information from sources that reinforce our beliefs and cut off sources that do not.

Motivated reasoning
Tendency to seek out information that supports what we want to believe.

Postmodernism
Any of a set of beliefs associated with a movement in art, architecture, music, and literature that tend to discount the idea of objective truth and a politically neutral frame of evaluation.

Post-truth
Contention that feelings are more accurate than facts, for the purpose of the political subordination of reality.

Prestige press
The "mainstream" newspapers in America, normally thought to include the *New York Times*, the *Wall Street Journal*, the *Washington Post*, and the *Los Angeles Times*.

Chapter 1

1. See Ashley Parker, "Donald Trump, Slipping in Polls, Warns of 'Stolen Election,'" *New York Times*, Oct. 13, 2016, https://www.nytimes.com/2016/10/14/us/politics/trump-election-rigging.html. Note that "post-truth" was chosen as the word of the year even before the US presidential election results were announced, in response to a spike in usage after the Brexit vote in June and Trump's nomination by the Republican Party in July. Amy B. Want, "'Post-Truth' named 2016 Word of the Year by Oxford Dictionaries," *Washington Post*, Nov. 16, 2016, https://www.washingtonpost.com/news/the-fix/wp/2016/11/16/post-truth-named-2016-word-of-the-year-by-oxford-dictionaries/?utm_term=.ff63c5e994c2.

2. See Michael D. Shear and Emmarie Huetteman, "Trump Repeats Lie about Popular Vote in Meeting with Lawmakers," *New York Times*, Jan. 23, 2017, https://www.nytimes.com/2017/01/23/us/politics/donald-trump-congress-democrats.html; Andy Greenberg, "A Timeline of Trump's Strange, Contradictory Statements on Russian Hacking," *Wired*, Jan. 4, 2017, https://www.wired.com/2017/01/timeline-trumps-strange-contradictory-statements-russian-hacking/.

3. Scottie Nell Hughes on *The Diane Rehm Show*, National Public Radio, Nov. 30, 2016, http://talkingpointsmemo.com/livewire/scottie-nell-hughes-there-are-no-more-facts.

4. See William Cummings, "Trump Falsely Claims Biggest Electoral Win since Reagan," *USA Today*, Feb. 16, 2017, https://www.usatoday.com/story/news/politics/onpolitics/2017/02/16/trump-falsely-claims-biggest-electoral-win-since-reagan/98002648/; Elle Hunt, "Trump's Inauguration Crowd: Sean Spicer's Claims versus the Evidence," *Guardian*, Jan. 22, 2017, https://www.theguardian.com/us-news/2017/jan/22/trump-inauguration-crowd-sean-spicers-claims-versus-the-evidence; S. V. Date, "Of Course the CIA Gave Trump Standing Ovations: He Never Let Them Sit," *Huffington Post*, Jan. 23, 2017, http://www.huffingtonpost.com/entry/trump-cia-ovations_us_58866825e4b0e3a7356b183f; Jeremy Diamond, "Trump Falsely Claims US Murder Rate Is 'Highest' in 47 Years," *CNN.com*, http://www.cnn.com/2017/02/07/politics/donald-trump-murder-rate-fact-check/index.html.

5. http://transcripts.cnn.com/TRANSCRIPTS/1607/22/nday.06.html.

6. In response to the selection of "post-truth" as 2016's word of the year, Stephen Colbert said that he was "pre-enraged. First of all, 'post-truth' is not a word of the year, it's the two words of the year. Hyphens are for the weak. Second, post-truth is clearly just a ripoff of my 2006 word of the year: truthiness." http://www.complex.com/pop-culture/2016/11/stephen-colbert-oxford-dictionary-post-truth-truthiness-rip-off.

7. Jon Henley, "Why Vote Leave's £350m Weekly EU Cost Claim Is Wrong," *Guardian*, June 10, 2016, https://www.theguardian.com/politics/reality-check/2016/may/23/does-the-eu-really-cost-the-uk-350m-a-week.

8. Eric Bradner, "Conway: Trump White House Offered 'Alternative Facts' on Crowd Size," *CNN.com*, Jan. 23, 2017, http://www.cnn.com/2017/01/22/politics/kellyanne-conway-alternative-facts/index.html.

9. Aristotle, *Metaphysics*, 1011b25.

10. For those interested in reading more on the fascinating subject of epistemology—the study of the theory of knowledge—perhaps the best place to start is Harry Frankfurt's erudite but accessible *On Truth* (New York: Knopf, 2006). For a bit more detail about the various theories of truth, one might turn to Frederick F. Schmitt, ed., *Theories of Truth* (New York: Wiley-Blackwell, 2003).

11. Shear and Huetteman, "Trump Repeats Lie," https://www.nytimes.com/2017/01/23/us/politics/donald-trump-congress-democrats.html. See also the story two days later reflecting on this milestone: Dan Barry, "In a Swirl of 'Untruths' and "Falsehoods,' Calling a Lie a Lie," *New York Times*, Jan. 25, 2017, https://www.nytimes.com/2017/01/25/business/media/donald-trump-lie-media.html. This was not, however, the first time that the *New York Times* had said Trump lied. See "'New York Times' Editor: 'We Owed It to Our Readers' to Call Trump Claims Lies," NPR.org, http://www.npr.org/2016/09/22/494919548/new-york-times-editor-we-owed-it-to-our-readers-to-call-trump-claims-lies.

12. Sarah Boseley, "Mbeki AIDS Denial 'Caused 300,000 Deaths,'" *Guardian*, Nov. 26, 2008, https://www.theguardian.com/world/2008/nov/26/aids-south-africa.

13. Louise Jacobson, "Yes Donald Trump Did Call Climate Change a Chinese Hoax," *Politifact*, June 3, 2016, http://www.politifact.com/truth-o-meter/statements/2016/jun/03/hillary-clinton/yes-donald-trump-did-call-climate-change-chinese-h/.

14. This claim has been made most prominently by Ted Cruz, who likes to claim that the NOAA's own data disprove the case for climate change, even while the study he cites has since been corrected: see Chris Mooney, "Ted Cruz's Favorite Argument about Climate Change Just Got Weaker," *Washington Post*, March 7, 2016, https://www.washingtonpost.com/news/energy

-environment/wp/2016/03/07/ted-cruzs-favorite-argument-about-climate
-change-just-got-weaker/?utm_term=.fb8b15b68e30.

15. One glaring example was seen in press secretary Sean Spicer's presentation of the March 2017 unemployment rate as 4.7 percent. When challenged
by reporters that Trump had dismissed such statistics as "phony" in the past
(when they favored Obama), Spicer laughed and said that Trump had told him
that if he got this question he was to say that such statistics "may have been
phony in the past, but it's very real now." Lauren Thomas, "White House's
Spicer: Trump Says Jobs Report 'May Have Been Phony in the Past, But It's
Very Real Now," *CNBC.com*, March 10, 2017, http://www.cnbc.com/2017/
03/10/white-houses-spicer-trump-says-jobs-report-may-have-been-phony
-in-the-past-but-its-very-real-now.html.

16. Lee McIntyre, *Respecting Truth: Willful Ignorance in the Internet Age* (New
York: Routledge, 2015).

Chapter 2

1. In his recent book *The Death of Expertise* (New York: Oxford University
Press, 2017), Tom Nichols explains that this is part of a growing phenomenon,
where laypersons are increasingly willing to challenge experts. In a recent radio
interview, he colorfully characterized it using a common exchange when people find out he is an authority on Russia. "You know a lot about Russia? Well
let me explain Russia to you." "One National Security Professor Alarmed by
'The Death of Expertise,'" WBUR.org, http://www.wbur.org/hereandnow/
2017/03/13/expertise-death-tom-nichols.

2. McIntyre, *Respecting Truth*, 8–9.

3. It is important to realize, though, that scientific confirmation is not an "all
or nothing" phenomenon. There are degrees of confirmation that can be assessed by the conformity of a theory with the evidence, but also with prior
probabilities. One way of doing this is through Bayesian inference, but there
are other methods as well. Given this, science *can* discount alternative theories, even if they are not strictly speaking "refuted," simply because they are
overwhelmingly unlikely to be true.

4. Again, the point here is that some scientific theories are more believable
than others, given the evidence. It is a logically absurd standard to say that one
must "prove" an empirical theory for one to be justified in believing it.

5. James Hansen, *Storms of My Grandchildren* (New York: Bloomsbury, 2011);
James Hoggan, *Climate Cover-Up: The Crusade to Deny Global Warming* (Van-
couver: Greystone, 2009); Chris Mooney, *The Republican War on Science* (New
York: Basic Books, 2005).

6. Ari Rabin-Havt, *Lies, Incorporated: The World of Post-Truth Politics* (New York: Anchor Books, 2016).

7. Naomi Oreskes and Erik Conway, *Merchants of Doubt: How a Handful of Scientists Obscured the Truth on Issues from Tobacco Smoke to Global Warming* (New York: Bloomsbury, 2010). Note that in 1964 the TIRC was succeeded by the Council for Tobacco Research.

8. Oreskes and Conway, *Merchants of Doubt*, 14–16; Rabin-Havt, *Lies, Incorporated*, 23–25.

9. It is a foundation of statistical reasoning that correlation does not equal causation. No matter how high the degree of correlation, it is unsound to infer that one thing *must* cause another. Again, we are back to the issue of "proof." High correlation certainly make it *more likely* that two variables are causally related, but anytime we are dealing with empirical matters, there is always going to be an element of doubt. One good resource for understanding this is Ronald Giere, *Understanding Scientific Reasoning* (New York: Harcourt, 1991).

10. Rabin-Havt, *Lies, Incorporated*, 26–27; see also Oreskes and Conway, *Merchants of Doubt*, 16.

11. Oreskes and Conway, *Merchants of Doubt*, 15, 33.

12. Ibid., 168.

13. Ibid., 34.

14. Ibid., 35.

15. Rabin-Havt, *Lies, Incorporated*, 7.

16. Oreskes and Conway, *Merchants of Doubt*, 234.

17. In 2012, Heartland's fundraising plan was leaked to the media, though they dispute the authenticity of some of the documents. See Richard Littlemore, "Heartland Insider Exposes Institute's Budget and Strategy," *Desmog*, Feb. 14, 2012, https://www.desmogblog.com/heartland-insider-exposes-institute-s-budget-and-strategy; https://s3.amazonaws.com/s3.documentcloud.org/documents/292934/1-15-2012-2012-fundraising-plan.pdf; Suzanne Goldenberg, "Leak Exposes How Heartland Institute Works to Undermine Climate Science," *Guardian*, Feb. 14, 2012, https://www.theguardian.com/environment/2012/feb/15/leak-exposes-heartland-institute-climate.

18. Juliet Eilperin, "Climate Skeptics Target State Energy Laws, Including Maine's," *Bangor Daily News*, Nov. 25, 2012, http://bangordailynews.com/2012/11/25/politics/climate-skeptics-target-state-energy-laws-including-maines/.

19. Though there is some question in the media lately over whether ExxonMobil has actually followed through on this pledge. Alexander Kaufman, "Exxon Continued Paying Millions to Climate-Change Deniers under Rex

Tillerson," *Huffington Post*, Jan. 9, 2017, http://www.huffingtonpost.com/entry/tillerson-exxon-climate-donations_us_5873a3f4e4b043ad97e48f52.

20. Steve Coll, *Private Empire: ExxonMobil and American Power* (New York: Penguin, 2012); "ExxonMobil: A 'Private Empire' on the World Stage," NPR.org, May 2, 2012, http://www.npr.org/2012/05/02/151842205/exxonmobil-a -private-empire-on-the-world-stage.

21. https://www.heartland.org/Center-Climate-Environment/index.html.

22. Justin Gillis and Leslie Kaufman, "Leak Offers Glimpse of Campaign against Climate Science," *New York Times*, Feb. 15, 2012, http://www.nytimes .com/2012/02/16/science/earth/in-heartland-institute-leak-a-plan-to-dis credit-climate-teaching.html.

23. Rabin-Havt, *Lies, Incorporated*, 42.

24. Ibid., 38.

25. Mooney, *The Republican War on Science*, 81.

26. https://www.desmogblog.com/2012/11/15/why-climate-deniers-have -no-credibility-science-one-pie-chart.

27. Rabin-Havt, *Lies, Incorporated*, 40. What about the remaining 3 percent? A later investigation found methodological errors in virtually *all* the contrarian studies on climate change. Dana Nuccitelli, "Here's What Happens When You Try to Replicate Climate Contrarian Studies," *Guardian*, Aug. 25, 2015, https://www.theguardian.com/environment/climate-consensus-97-per -cent/2015/aug/25/heres-what-happens-when-you-try-to-replicate-climate -contrarian-papers.

28. http://www.pewinternet.org/2016/10/04/the-politics-of-climate/.

29. Rabin-Havt, *Lies, Incorporated*, 34.

30. John H. Cushman Jr., "Industrial Group Plans to Battle Climate Treaty," *New York Times*, April 26, 1998, http://www.nytimes.com/1998/04/26/us/ industrial-group-plans-to-battle-climate-treaty.html.

31. The material for this quotation is no longer available from its original source (http://www.euronet.nl/users/e_wesker/ew@shell/API-prop.html). It has, however, been quoted in several other publications, including James Hoggan and Richard Littlemore, *Climate Cover-Up: The Crusade to Deny Global Warming* (Vancouver: Greystone, 2009), 43.

32. There is evidence that this is already happening and that perhaps the tobacco strategy is now being used on the murder rate. Although experts agree that the murder rate is near a historic low, public opinion shows an increasing belief that it is high. Tristan Bridges, "There's an Intriguing Sociological Reason So Many Americans Are Ignoring Facts Lately," *Business Insider*, Feb. 27, 2017, http://www.businessinsider.com/sociology-alternative-facts-2017-2.

Chapter 3

1. For more on the idea that there are many ways to accommodate even rational beliefs, see W. V. O. Quine and J. S. Ullian, *The Web of Belief* (New York: McGraw Hill, 1978).

2. Solomon Asch, "Opinions and Social Pressure," *Scientific American*, Nov. 1955, 3, http://kosmicki.com/102/Asch1955.pdf.

3. For those who don't already know, confirmation bias is when we seek out information that confirms what we already believe.

4. P. C. Wason, "On the Failure to Eliminate Hypotheses in a Conceptual Task," *Quarterly Journal of Experimental Psychology* 12 (1960): 129–140, http://web.mit.edu/curhan/www/docs/Articles/biases/12_Quarterly_J_Experimental_Psychology_129_(Wason).pdf.

5. In his delightful book *Thinking Fast and Slow* (New York: Farrar, Straus & Giroux, 2011), Daniel Kahneman gives a definitive and readable account of his life's work on these issues.

6. See https://en.wikipedia.org/wiki/List_of_cognitive_biases.

7. Juliet Macur, "Why Do Fans Excuse the Patriots' Cheating Past?" *New York Times*, Feb. 5, 2017; David DeSteno and Piercarlo Valdesolo, "Manipulations of Emotional Context Shape Moral Judgment," *Psychological Science* 17, no. 6 (2006): 476–477.

8. Drew Westen et al., "Neural Bases of Motivated Reasoning: An fMRI Study of Emotional Constraints on Partisan Political Judgment in the 2004 U.S. Presidential Election," *Journal of Cognitive Neuroscience* 18, no. 11 (November 2006): 1947–1958.

9. Brendan Nyhan and Jason Reifler, "When Corrections Fail: The Persistence of Political Misperceptions," *Political Behavior* 32, no. 2 (June 2010): 303–330, https://www.dartmouth.edu/~nyhan/nyhan-reifler.pdf.

10. Ibid.

11. Tristan Bridges, "There's an Intriguing Reason so Many Americans Are Ignoring Facts Lately," *Business Insider* (Feb. 27, 2017), http://www.businessinsider.com/sociology-alternative-facts-2017-2.

12. David Redlawsk et al. "The Affective Tipping Point: Do Motivated Reasoners Ever 'Get It'?" http://rci.rutgers.edu/~redlawsk/papers/A%20Tipping%20Point%20Final%20Version.pdf. In the meantime, further neurological studies have suggested that we use different parts of our brain to process "contradicting" information. See Jonas Kaplan, Sarah Gimbel, and Sam Harris, "Neural Correlates of Maintaining One's Political Beliefs in the Face of Counterevidence," *Scientific Reports* 6, http://www.nature.com/articles/srep39589.

13. Justin Kruger and David Dunning, "Unskilled and Unaware of It: How Difficulties in Recognizing One's Own Incompetence Lead to Inflated Self-Assessments," *Journal of Personality and Social Psychology* 77, no. 6 (1999): 1121, http://psych.colorado.edu/~vanboven/teaching/p7536_heur bias/p7536_readings/kruger_dunning.pdf.

14. Ibid., 1125.

15. Natalie Wolchover, "Incompetent People Too Ignorant to Know It," *Live Science*, Feb. 27, 2012, http://www.livescience.com/18678-incompetent-people -ignorant.html.

16. Ted Barrett, "Inhofe Brings Snowball on Senate Floor as Evidence Globe Is Not Warming," *CNN.com*, Feb. 27, 2015, http://www.cnn.com/2015/02/ 26/politics/james-inhofe-snowball-climate-change/index.html; https://www .facebook.com/cnn/videos/10154213275786509. Some have already started to call Donald Trump the Dunning–Kruger president. Jessica Pressler, "Donald Trump, the Dunning–Kruger President," *NYmag.com*, Jan. 9, 2017, http:// nymag.com/scienceofus/2017/01/why-donald-trump-will-be-the-dunning -kruger-president.html.

17. There is currently a furious academic debate on this subject. See Hugo Mercier and Daniel Sperber, "Why Do Humans Reason? Arguments for an Argumentative Theory," *Behavioral and Brain Sciences* 34, no. 2 (2011): 57–111. I discuss this debate in chapter 2 of my *Respecting Truth*.

18. Daniel Fessler et al., "Political Orientation Predicts Credulity Regarding Putative Hazards," http://www.danielmtfessler.com/wp-content/uploads/ 2013/12/Fessler-et-al-in-press-Political-Orientation-Credulity.pdf.

19. Olga Khazan, "Why Fake News Targeted Trump Supporters," *Atlantic*, Feb. 2, 2017, https://www.theatlantic.com/science/archive/2017/02/why-fake -news-targeted-trump-supporters/515433.

20. Ryota Kanai et al., "Political Orientations Are Correlated with Brain Structure in Young Adults," *Current Biology* 21, no. 8 (April 26, 2011): 677–680, https://www.ncbi.nlm.nih.gov/pmc/articles/PMC3092984/.

21. Melissa Healy, "Why Conservatives Are More Likely Than Liberals to Believe False Information about Threats," *Los Angeles Times*, Feb. 2, 2017, http:// www.latimes.com/science/sciencenow/la-sci-sn-conservative-believe-false -threats-20170202-story.html.

22. Ibid.

23. Cass Sunstein, *Infotopia: How Many Minds Produce Knowledge* (Oxford: Oxford University Press, 2006).

24. It is important to note that this was not due to the "smartest person in the room" phenomenon, where one person figured it out and told the group the

answer. Also, it was not the mere "wisdom of crowds" effect, which relies on passive majority opinion. The effect was found only when group members interacted with one another.

25. Khazan, "Why Fake News Targeted Trump Supporters," https://www.theatlantic.com/science/archive/2017/02/why-fake-news-targeted-trump-supporters/515433/; Christopher Ingraham, "Why Conservatives Might Be More Likely to Fall for Fake News," *Washington Post*, Dec. 7, 2016, https://www.washingtonpost.com/news/wonk/wp/2016/12/07/why-conservatives-might-be-more-likely-to-fall-for-fake-news/?utm_term=.eab87fe90c63.

Chapter 4

1. "Sixty Years of Daily Newspapers Circulation Trends," May 6, 2011, http://media-cmi.com/downloads/Sixty_Years_Daily_Newspaper_Circulation_Trends_050611.pdf.

2. Or by an anchorwoman; Barbara Walters joined ABC News as coanchor in 1976.

3. David Halberstam, *The Powers That Be* (Urbana: University of Illinois Press, 2000), xi.

4. Ted Koppel, "Olbermann, O'Reilly and the Death of Real News," *Washington Post*, Nov. 14, 2010, http://www.washingtonpost.com/wp-dyn/content/article/2010/11/12/AR2010111202857.html.

5. Ibid., 2. See also Marc Gunther, "The Transformation of Network News," *Nieman Reports*, June 15, 1999, http://niemanreports.org/articles/the-transformation-of-network-news/: "[Roone Arledge, President of ABC News] saw no reason why news couldn't make a profit"; "'When I came here, we were losing money in news and that was thought of as an acceptable situation,' recalls Bob Wright, who has been NBC's Chief Executive Officer since GE bought the network in 1986."

6. Nichols, *The Death of Expertise: The Campaign against Established Knowledge and Why It Matters* (Oxford: Oxford University Press, 2017), 149–150.

7. Sandra Salmans, "Television's 'Bad Boy' Makes Good," *New York Times*, Aug. 14, 1983, http://www.nytimes.com/1983/08/14/business/television-s-bad-boy-makes-good.html?pagewanted=all.

8. http://www.pophistorydig.com/topics/ted-turner-cnn-1980s-1990s/.

9. Nichols, *The Death of Expertise*, 146.

10. Ibid.

11. Ibid., 153.

12. Jack Mirkinson, "Fox News Execs Squashed Talk of Gun Control after Newtown Massacre: Report," *Huffington Post*, Dec. 17, 2012, http://www.huff

ingtonpost.com/2012/12/17/fox-news-gun-control-sandy-hook-newtown _n_2318431.html.

13. Cenk Uygur, "Will John Moody Be Forced Out of Fox Like Dan Rather from CBS?" *Huffington Post*, Nov. 15, 2006, http://www.huffingtonpost.com/cenk -uygur/will-john-moody-be-forced_b_34162.html.

14. Shauna Theel, Max Greenberg, and Denise Robbins, "Study: Media Sowed Doubt in Coverage of UN Climate Report," *Media Matters*, Oct. 10, 2013, https://mediamatters.org/research/2013/10/10/study-media-sowed-doubt -in-coverage-of-un-clima/196387.

15. http://www.stateofthemedia.org/2005/cable-tv-intro/content-analysis/.

16. http://publicmind.fdu.edu/2011/knowless/.

17. Koppel, "Olbermann, O'Reilly and the Death of Real News."

18. Daniel Politi, "Watch Ted Koppel Tell Sean Hannity He's Bad for America, *Slate*, March 26, 2017, http://www.slate.com/blogs/the_slatest/2017/03/26/ watch_ted_koppel_tell_sean_hannity_he_s_bad_for_america.html.

19. MSNBC came in last at 10 percent. Citation from Nichols, *The Death of Expertise*, 155–156.

20. http://transcripts.cnn.com/TRANSCRIPTS/0410/15/cf.01.html.

21. Stephen Marche, "The Left Has a Post-Truth Problem Too: It's Called Comedy," *Los Angeles Times*, Jan. 6, 2017, http://www.latimes.com/opinion/op-ed/ la-oe-marche-left-fake-news-problem-comedy-20170106-story.html.

22. Ibid.

23. Ibid.

24. "The White House and the Green House," *New York Times*, May 9, 1989, http://www.nytimes.com/1989/05/09/opinion/the-white-house-and-the -greenhouse.html.

25. James Hansen, "The Threat to the Planet," *New York Review of Books*, July 13, 2006, http://www.nybooks.com/articles/2006/07/13/the-threat-to-the -planet/.

26. Brent Cunningham, "Rethinking Objectivity," *Columbia Journalism Review*, July–August 2003, http://archives.cjr.org/feature/rethinking_object ivity.php.

27. Donald Trump with Tony Schwartz, *The Art of the Deal* (New York: Random House, 1992).

28. Steven Salzberg, "Anti-Vaccine Movement Causes Worst Measles Epidemic in 20 Years," Forbes.com, Feb. 1, 2015, https://www.forbes.com/sites/ stevensalzberg/2015/02/01/anti-vaccine-movement-causes-worst-measles -epidemic-in-20-years/#27ce10b6069d.

29. Maxwell Boykoff and Jules Boykoff, "Balance as Bias: Global Warming and the US Prestige Press," *Global Environmental Change* 14 (2004): 125–136, http://sciencepolicy.colorado.edu/admin/publication_files/2004.33.pdf.

30. Ibid., 127.

31. Ibid.

32. Ibid., 129.

33. Ibid., 129.

34. Ibid.

35. There is some good news to report here. Since Trump's election subscriptions to the *New York Times*, the *Los Angeles Times*, and the *Washington Post* are all up. The *Washington Post* announced in December, 2016, that it would be adding sixty newsroom jobs. Laurel Wamsley, "Big Newspapers Are Booming: 'Washington Post' to Add 60 Newsroom Jobs," NPR.org, http://www.npr.org/sections/thetwo-way/2016/12/27/507140760/big-newspapers-are-booming-washington-post-to-add-sixty-newsroom-jobs.

36. Julie Hirschfeld Davis and Matthew Rosenberg, "With False Claims, Trump Attacks Media on Turnout and Intelligence Rift," *New York Times*, Jan. 21, 2017, https://www.nytimes.com/2017/01/21/us/politics/trump-white-house-briefing-inauguration-crowd-size.html.

37. http://www.gallup.com/poll/195542/americans-trust-mass-media-sinks-new-low.aspx.

38. "Professor Makes List of Fake, Misleading News Sites You May Want to Avoid," CBS Boston, Nov. 16, 2016, http://boston.cbslocal.com/2016/11/16/fake-news-sites-websites-list-professor-merrimack-college-zimdars/.

Chapter 5

1. Katharine Seelye, "Newspaper Circulation Falls Sharply," *New York Times*, Oct. 31, 2006, http://www.nytimes.com/2006/10/31/business/media/31paper.html.

2. Richard Perez-Pena, "Newspaper Circulation Continues to Decline Rapidly," *New York Times*, Oct. 27, 2008, http://www.nytimes.com/2008/10/28/business/media/28circ.html.

3. Pew Research Center, "State of the News Media 2016: Newspapers Fact Sheet," June 15, 2016, http://www.journalism.org/2016/06/15/newspapers-fact-sheet/.

4. Lucinda Fleeson, "Bureau of Missing Bureaus," *American Journalism Review* (Oct.–Nov. 2003), http://ajrarchive.org/Article.asp?id=3409.

5. Paul Farhl, "One Billion Dollars Profit? Yes, the Campaign Has Been a Gusher for CNN," *Washington Post*, Oct. 27, 2016, https://www.washington

post.com/lifestyle/style/one-billion-dollars-profit-yes-the-campaign-has
-been-a-gusher-for-cnn/2016/10/27/1fc879e6-9c6f-11e6-9980-50913
d68eacb_story.html?utm_term=.c00743f7897c.

6. Ibid.

7. Brett Edkins, "Donald Trump's Election Delivers Massive Ratings for Cable
News," *Forbes*, Dec. 1, 2016, https://www.forbes.com/sites/brettedkins/2016/
12/01/donald-trumps-election-delivers-massive-ratings-for-cable
-news/#3df398f5119e.

8. Neal Gabler, "Donald Trump Triggers a Media Civil War," billmoyers
.com, March 25, 2016, http://billmoyers.com/story/donald-trump-triggers-a
-media-civil-war/.

9. Rantt Editorial Board, "The Media Helped Elect Donald Trump and They
Need to Own Up to It," rantt.com, Dec. 20, 2016, https://rantt.com/the
-media-helped-elect-donald-trump-and-they-need-to-own-up-to-it-a33804
e9cf1a.

10. Ibid.

11. Ibid.

12. Jeffrey Gottfried and Elisa Shearer, Pew Research Center, "News Use
across Social Media Platforms 2016," journalism.org, May 26, 2016, http://
www.journalism.org/files/2016/05/PJ_2016.05.26_social-media-and-news
_FINAL.pdf.

13. Ricardo Gandour, "Study: Decline of Traditional Media Feeds Polarization," *Columbia Journalism Review*, Sept. 19, 2016, http://www.cjr.org/analy
sis/media_polarization_journalism.php.

14. Jacob Soll, "The Long and Brutal History of Fake News," *Politico*, Dec. 18,
2016, http://www.politico.com/magazine/story/2016/12/fake-news-history
-long-violent-214535.

15. Ibid.

16. Ibid.

17. Michael Schudson, *Discovering the News: A Social History of American Newspapers* (New York: Basic Books, 1981), 4. Note here a dispute with Soll over
when the concept of "news" was invented. Schudson says that the concept of
news began in the Jacksonian era; Soll says that "news became a concept 500
years ago with the invention of print."

18. Ibid.

19. Ibid., 5.

20. Christopher Woolf, "Back in the 1890s, Fake News Helped Start a War,"
Public Radio International, Dec. 8, 2016, https://www.pri.org/stories/2016-12
-08/long-and-tawdry-history-yellow-journalism-america.

21. Quotation by Joseph E. Wisan (1934), cited from Alexandra Samuel, "To Fix Fake News, Look to Yellow Journalism," *JSTOR Daily*, Nov. 29, 2016, https://daily.jstor.org/to-fix-fake-news-look-to-yellow-journalism/.

22. Soll, "The Long and Brutal History."

23. Woolf, "Back in the 1890s, Fake News Helped Start a War."

24. Schudson, *Discovering the News*, 5.

25. Soll, "The Long and Brutal History."

26. Jason Stanley, "The Truth about Post-Truth," *Ideas with Paul Kennedy*, Canadian Broadcasting Corporation Radio, April 17, 2017, http://www.cbc.ca/radio/ideas/the-truth-about-post-truth-1.3939958.

27. Perhaps an analogy with lying will help to understand that it is the intention to mislead—rather than the mere falsehood of its content—that makes fake news fake. Though this does raise the question: what if the person sharing an untruth actually believes it? Then is it fake? Is Trump inoculated if he is deluded enough to think that he actually won the popular vote?

28. Andrew Higgins et al., "Inside a Fake News Sausage Factory: 'This Is All About Income,'" *New York Times*, Nov. 25, 2016, https://www.nytimes.com/2016/11/25/world/europe/fake-news-donald-trump-hillary-clinton-georgia.html?_r=0.

29. Ibid.

30. Samantha Subramanian, "Inside the Macedonian Fake-News Complex," *Wired*, Feb. 15, 2017, https://www.wired.com/2017/02/veles-macedonia-fake-news/.

31. Scott Shane, "From Headline to Photograph, a Fake News Masterpiece," *New York Times*, Jan. 18, 2017, https://www.nytimes.com/2017/01/18/us/fake-news-hillary-clinton-cameron-harris.html.

32. Joe Marusak, "Fake News Author Is Fired; Apologizes to Those Who Are 'Disappointed' by His Actions," *Charlotte Observer*, Jan. 19, 2017, http://www.charlotteobserver.com/news/local/article127391619.html.

33. On March 31, 2017, the US Senate Intelligence Committee announced that it was looking into "reports that Russia hired at least 1000 trolls to spread fake news stories to hurt Democratic candidate Hillary Clinton during the presidential election." http://www.huffingtonpost.com/entry/russian-trolls-fake-news_us_58dde6bae4b08194e3b8d5c4. Apparently the effort was so sophisticated that it was able to target specific swing states like Wisconsin, Michigan, and Pennsylvania. http://www.independent.co.uk/news/world/americas/us-politics/russian-trolls-hilary-clinton-fake-news-election-democrat-mark-warner-intelligence-committee-a7657641.html.

34. Sapna Maheshwari, "How Fake News Goes Viral: A Case Study," *New York Times*, Nov. 20, 2016, https://www.nytimes.com/2016/11/20/business/media/how-fake-news-spreads.html?_r=0.

35. "Man Opens Fire in Restaurant Targeted by Anti-Clinton 'Pizzagate' Fake News Conspiracy," CBS News, Dec. 4, 2016, http://www.cbsnews.com/news/police-man-with-assault-rifle-dc-comet-pizza-victim-of-fake-sex-trafficking-story/.

36. Craig Silverman, "This Analysis Shows How Viral Fake Election News Stories Outperformed Real News on Facebook," buzzfeed.com, Nov. 16, 2016, https://www.buzzfeed.com/craigsilverman/viral-fake-election-news-outperformed-real-news-on-facebook?utm_term=.lrJLPJLWV#.ssvv6Avgl.

37. "Duped by Fake News, Pakistan Defense Minister Makes Nuke Threat to Israel," yahoo.com, Dec. 26, 2016, https://www.yahoo.com/news/duped-fake-news-pakistan-minister-makes-nuke-threat-074808075.html.

38. Sam Kestenbaum, "Google 'Did the Holocaust Happen'—and a Neo-Nazi Site Is the Top Hit," forward.com, Dec. 13, 2016, http://forward.com/news/356923/google-did-the-holocaust-happen-and-a-neo-nazi-site-is-the-top-hit/.

39. Philip Bump, "Google's Top News Link for 'Final Election Results' Goes to a Fake News Site with False Numbers," *Washington Post*, Nov. 14, 2016, https://www.washingtonpost.com/news/the-fix/wp/2016/11/14/googles-top-news-link-for-final-election-results-goes-to-a-fake-news-site-with-false-numbers/?utm_term=.a75261b0dea8.

40. Danielle Kurtzleben, "With 'Fake News,' Trump Moves from Alternative Facts to Alternative Language," NPR.org, Feb. 17, 2017, http://www.npr.org/2017/02/17/515630467/with-fake-news-trump-moves-from-alternative-facts-to-alternative-language.

41. Jason Stanley, *How Propaganda Works* (Princeton, NJ: Princeton University Press, 2015).

42. "How Propaganda Works in the Age of Fake News," WBUR.org, Feb. 15, 2017, http://www.wbur.org/hereandnow/2017/02/15/how-propaganda-works-fake-news.

43. Much the same point is made by Julie Beck in her article "This Article Won't Change Your Mind," *Atlantic*, March 13, 2017, https://www.theatlantic.com/science/archive/2017/03/this-article-wont-change-your-mind/519093/.

44. Ron Suskind, "Faith, Certainty and the Presidency of George W. Bush," *New York Times Magazine*, Oct. 17, 2004, http://www.nytimes.com/2004/10/

17/magazine/faith-certainty-and-the-presidency-of-george-w-bush.html?
_r=0.

45. Hannah Arendt, *The Origins of Totalitarianism* (New York: Harcourt, Brace, 1951), 474.

46. Charles Simic, "Expendable America," *New York Review of Books*, Nov. 19, 2016, http://www.nybooks.com/daily/2016/11/19/trump-election -expendable-america/.

47. Timothy Snyder, *On Tyranny: Twenty Lessons from the 20th Century* (New York: Tim Duggan Books, 2017).

48. Sean Illing, "'Post-Truth Is Pre-Fascism': A Holocaust Historian on the Trump Era," *Vox*, March 9, 2017, http://www.vox.com/conversations/2017/ 3/9/14838088/donald-trump-fascism-europe-history-totalitarianism -post-truth.

49. http://www.marketwatch.com/story/how-does-your-favorite-news -source-rate-on-the-truthiness-scale-consult-this-chart-2016-12-15.

50. Robinson Meyer, "The Rise of Progressive 'Fake News,'" *Atlantic*, Feb. 3, 2017, https://www.theatlantic.com/technology/archive/2017/02/viva-la -resistance-content/515532/; Sam Levin, "Fake News for Liberals: Misinfor- mation Starts to Lean Left under Trump," *Guardian*, Feb. 6, 2017, https://www .theguardian.com/media/2017/feb/06/liberal-fake-news-shift-trump -standing-rock.

51. Katharine Viner, "How Technology Disrupted the Truth," *Guardian*, July 12, 2016, https://www.theguardian.com/media/2016/jul/12/how-tech nology-disrupted-the-truth.

52. Nick Wingfield et al., "Google and Facebook Take Aim at Fake News Sites," *New York Times*, Nov. 14, 2016, https://www.nytimes.com/2016/11/15/tech nology/google-will-ban-websites-that-host-fake-news-from-using-its-ad -service.html.

53. Ibid.

54. David Pierson, "Facebook Bans Fake News from Its Advertising Net- work—but not Its News Feed," *Los Angeles Times*, Nov. 15, 2016, http://www .latimes.com/business/la-fi-facebook-fake-news-20161115-story.html. Yet in September 2017, Facebook revealed it had sold thousands of ads to a Russian company with links to the Kremlin, which were intended to manipulate the 2016 presidential election. Scott Shane and Vindu Goel, "Fake Russian Face- book Accounts Bought $100,000 in Political Ads," *New York Times*, Sept. 6, 2017, https://www.nytimes.com/2017/09/06/technology/facebook-russian -political-ads.html.

55. Pierson, "Facebook Bans Fake News."

56. Facebook now has a help page called "Tips to Spot False News," which is helpful but still leaves the responsibility mostly on viewers to purge their own news feeds of fake news content. https://techcrunch.com/2017/04/06/facebook-puts-link-to-10-tips-for-spotting-false-news-atop-feed/.

57. Quoted in Meyer, "The Rise of Progressive 'Fake News,'" https://www.theatlantic.com/technology/archive/2017/02/viva-la-resistance-content/515532/.

58. Laurel Wamsley, "Big Newspapers Are Booming: 'Washington Post' to Add 60 Newsroom Jobs," NPR.org, Dec. 27, 2016, http://www.npr.org/sections/thetwo-way/2016/12/27/507140760/big-newspapers-are-booming-washington-post-to-add-sixty-newsroom-jobs.

59. Daniel J. Levitin, *Weaponized Lies: How to Think Critically in the Post-Truth Era* (New York: Dutton, 2017).

60. Scott Bedley, "I Taught My 5th-Graders How to Spot Fake News: Now They Won't Stop Fact-Checking Me," *Vox*, May 29, 2017, http://www.vox.com/first-person/2017/3/29/15042692/fake-news-education-election.

Chapter 6

1. Michael Lynch, *True to Life: Why Truth Matters* (Cambridge, MA: MIT Press, 2004), 35–36.

2. Conor Lynch, "Trump's War on Environment and Science Are Rooted in His Post-Truth Politics—and Maybe in Postmodern Philosophy," *Salon*, April 1, 2017, http://www.salon.com/2017/04/01/trumps-war-on-environment-and-science-are-rooted-in-his-post-truth-politics-and-maybe-in-postmodern-philosophy/.

3. Paul Gross and Norman Levitt, *Higher Superstition: The Academic Left and Its Quarrels with Science* (Baltimore: Johns Hopkins University Press, 1994), 77.

4. Lynne Cheney, *Telling the Truth* (New York: Simon & Schuster, 1995).

5. For some excellent critiques of postmodernist thought, see Michael Lynch, *In Praise of Reason* (Cambridge, MA: MIT Press, 2012); Paul Boghossian, *Fear of Knowledge: Against Relativism and Constructivism* (Oxford: Clarendon Press, 2007); Noretta Koertge, ed., *A House Built on Sand: Exposing Postmodernist Myths about Science* (Oxford: Oxford University Press, 1998).

6. If one wishes to learn more about the "strong programme," and its founder David Bloor, one of the best places to start is a critical essay entitled "David Bloor and the Strong Programme," by Collin Finn, which appears as chapter 3 of his book *Science Studies as Naturalized Philosophy*, Synthese Library Book Series, vol. 348 (Springer, 2011), 35–62.

7. It seems ironic that in the latest (October 2016) Pew Poll on "The Politics of Climate Change" some of these claims seem to have been taken up by the far right. When asked to respond to the prompt that "climate scientists' research findings are influenced by _____ most of the time" it was found that 57 percent of conservative Republicans agreed with the idea that it was "scientist's desire to advance their careers," 54 percent agreed with "scientists' own political leanings," and only 9 percent agreed with "best available scientific evidence." http://www.pewinternet.org/2016/10/04/the-politics-of-climate/.

8. Carolyn Merchant, *The Death of Nature* (New York: Harper, 1990).

9. Sandra Harding, *The Science Question in Feminism* (Ithaca: Cornell University Press, 1986), 113.

10. If one wants to read a nuanced philosophical account that questions our traditional notions of objectivity yet defends the distinctiveness of science, see Helen Longino, *Science as Social Knowledge: Values and Objectivity in Scientific Inquiry* (Princeton, NJ: Princeton University Press, 1990).

11. Alan Sokal, "Transgressing the Boundaries: Toward a Transformative Hermeneutics of Quantum Gravity," *Social Text* 46–47 (spring–summer 1996): 217–252, http://www.physics.nyu.edu/sokal/transgress_v2_noafterword.pdf.

12. Alan Sokal, "A Physicist Experiments with Cultural Studies," *Lingua Franca* (May–June 1996), http://www.physics.nyu.edu/faculty/sokal/lingua_franca_v4/lingua_franca_v4.html.

13. Ibid.

14. Commenting on this, Michael Berube writes: "[Sokal] believed—and he was not alone—that postmodernism and theory were bad for the left, and that the academic wing of the left was aggressively undermining the foundations of progressive politics." Michael Berube, "The Science Wars Redux," *Democracy Journal* (winter 2011): 70.

15. Sokal, "A Physicist Experiments with Cultural Studies."

16. Judith Warner, "Fact-Free Science," *New York Times Magazine*, Feb. 25, 2011, http://www.nytimes.com/2011/02/27/magazine/27FOB-WWLN-t.html.

17. Chris Mooney, "Once and For All: Climate Denial Is Not Postmodern," *Desmog*, Feb. 28, 2011, https://www.desmogblog.com/once-and-all-climate-denial-not-postmodern.

18. Ibid.

19. Robert Pennock, "The Postmodern Sin of Intelligent Design Creationism," *Science and Education* 19 (2010): 757–778, https://msu.edu/~pennock5/research/papers/Pennock_PostmodernSinID.pdf.

20. J. Lawrence, interview with Phillip E. Johnson, *Communique: A Quarterly Journal* (Spring 1999), http://www.arn.org/docs/johnson/commsp99.htm.

21. G. Silberman, "Phil Johnson's Little Hobby," *Boalt Hall Cross-Examiner* 6, no. 2 (1993): 4.

22. P. Johnson, "Open Letter to John W. Burgeson." Pennock cites this as "published on the Internet" but it must have since been taken down. Citation is from Pennock, "The Postmodern Sin," 759.

23. N. Pearcey, "Anti-Darwinism Comes to the University: An Interview with Phillip Johnson," *Bible Science Newsletter* 28, no. 6 (1990): 11.

24. Pennock, "The Postmodern Sin," 762.

25. For a discussion of how the battle over intelligent design influenced the one over climate change, see my *Respecting Truth: Willful Ignorance in the Internet Age* (New York: Routledge, 2015), 56–80.

26. A few of these were cited by Warner in her 2011 piece. Mooney seems to have missed them.

27. http://www.nytimes.com/2003/03/15/opinion/environmental-word-games.html.

28. Bruno Latour, "Why Has Critique Run Out of Steam? From Matters of Fact to Matters of Concern," *Critical Inquiry* 30 (winter 2004): 225–248, http://www.unc.edu/clct/LatourCritique.pdf.

29. Ibid.

30. Michael Berube, "The Science Wars Redux," *Democracy Journal* (winter 2011): 64–74, http://democracyjournal.org/magazine/19/the-science-wars-redux/.

31. Ibid.

32. Conor Lynch, "Trump's War on Environment and Science Are Rooted in His Post-Truth Politics," http://www.salon.com/2017/04/01/trumps-war-on-environment-and-science-are-rooted-in-his-post-truth-politics-and-maybe-in-postmodern-philosophy/.

33. In "Why Has Critique Run Out of Steam?" Latour writes: "Of course, conspiracy theories are an absurd deformation of our own arguments, but, like weapons smuggled through a fuzzy border to the wrong party, these are our weapons nonetheless. In spite of all the deformations, it is easy to recognize, still burnt in the steel, our trademark" (230).

34. I raised the issue of whether postmodernism was one of the roots of science denial in my *Respecting Truth*, 104–107, and again in my article "The Attack on Truth," *Chronicle of Higher Education*, June 8, 2015, http://www.chronicle.com/article/The-Attack-on-Truth/230631. As I've argued in chapter 2 of the present book, I believe that science denial is a precursor to post-truth. When these two strands are taken together, it follows that postmodernism is also one of the roots of post-truth.

35. See the previously cited article by Conor Lynch, "Trump's War on Environment and Science Are Rooted in His Post-Truth Politics." See also Andrew Calcutt, "The Truth about Post-Truth Politics," *Newsweek*, Nov. 21, 2016, http://www.newsweek.com/truth-post-truth-politics-donald-trump-liberals-tony-blair-523198, and Andrew Jones, "Want to Better Understand 'Post-Truth' Politics? Then Study Postmodernism," *Huffington Post*, Nov. 11, 2016, http://www.huffingtonpost.co.uk/andrew-jones/want-to-better-understand_b_13079632.html. For a few interesting blog posts see "Donald Trump and the Triumph of Right-Wing Postmodernism," *Stewedrabbit* (blog), Dec. 12, 2016, http://stewedrabbit.blogspot.com/2016/12/donald-trump-and-triumph-of-right-wing.html, and Charles Kurzman, "Rightwing Postmodernists," Nov. 30, 2014, http://kurzman.unc.edu/rightwing-postmodernists/.

36. Truman Chen, "Is Postmodernism to Blame for Post-Truth?" *Philosophytalk* (blog), Feb. 17, 2017, https://www.philosophytalk.org/blog/postmodernism-blame-post-truth.

37. Ibid.

38. Carole Cadwalladr, "Daniel Dennett: 'I Begrudge Every Hour I Have to Spend Worrying about Politics,'" *Guardian*, Feb. 12, 2017, https://www.theguardian.com/science/2017/feb/12/daniel-dennett-politics-bacteria-bach-back-dawkins-trump-interview.

39. Although he does not identify himself as a member of the "alt-right," it was noted by one journalist that when Cernovich discusses the alt-right movement he says "we." Andrew Marantz, "Trolls for Trump: Meet Mike Cernovich, the Meme Mastermind of the Alt-Right," *New Yorker*, Oct. 31, 2016, http://www.newyorker.com/magazine/2016/10/31/trolls-for-trump.

40. Maxwell Tani, "Some of Trump's Top Supporters Are Praising a Conspiracy Theorist Who Fueled 'Pizzagate' for His Reporting," *Business Insider*, April 4, 2017, http://www.businessinsider.com/mike-cernovich-kellyanne-conway-donald-trump-jr-2017-4.

41. Gideon Resnick, "Trump's Son Says Mike 'Pizzagate' Cernovich Deserves a Pulitzer," *The Daily Beast*, April 4, 2017, http://www.thedailybeast.com/articles/2017/04/04/trump-s-son-says-mike-pizzagate-cernovich-deserves-a-pulitzer.html.

42. https://www.youtube.com/watch?v=4ZmljpEf4q4.

43. Abby Ohlheiser and Ben Terris, "How Mike Cernovich's Influence Moved from the Internet Fringes to the White House," *Washington Post*, April 7, 2017, https://www.washingtonpost.com/news/the-intersect/wp/2017/04/07/how-mike-cernovichs-influence-moved-from-the-internet-fringes-to-the-white-house/?utm_term=.1f0eca43415c.

44. For Cernovich's views on date rape, see Tani, "Some of Trump's Supporters." For his views on "feminist indoctrination," see Marantz, "Trolls for Trump." Also in Marantz's article: "In 2003, he [Cernovich] was accused of raping a woman he knew; the charge was later dropped, but a judge ordered him to do community service for misdemeanor battery" (4).

45. Cernovich critic Vic Berger, quoted in Tani, "Some of Trump's Supporters."

46. Marantz, "Trolls for Trump."

Chapter 7

1. Nancy Gibbs, "When a President Can't Be Taken at His Word," *Time*, April 3, 2017, http://time.com/4710615/donald-trump-truth-falsehoods/.

2. Ibid.

3. Farhad Manjoo, *True Enough: Learning to Live in a Post-Fact Society* (Hoboken, NJ: Wiley, 2008).

4. In 2004, Ralph Keyes published *The Post-Truth Era: Dishonesty and Deception in Contemporary Life* (New York: St. Martin's, 2004), which is concerned with lying and dishonesty as a societal problem. In 2015, I published *Respecting Truth: Willful Ignorance in the Internet Age* (New York: Routledge, 2015), in which I decried some then-unnamed "post-truth" tactics in the increasingly partisan "war on science." Neither of us, however, anticipated the jump to national politics in the way Manjoo did.

5. Manjoo, *True Enough*, 56–58.

6. Lindsay Abrams, "BBC Staff Ordered to Stop Giving Equal Airtime to Climate Deniers," *Salon*, July 6, 2014, http://www.salon.com/2014/07/06/bbc_staff_ordered_to_stop_giving_equal_air_time_to_climate_deniers/.

7. Justin Ellis, "Why the Huffington Post Doesn't Equivocate on Issues like Global Warming," *NiemanLab*, April 16, 2012, http://www.niemanlab.org/2012/04/why-the-huffington-post-doesnt-equivocate-on-issues-like-global-warming/.

8. David Redlawsk et al., "The Affective Tipping Point: Do Motivated Reasoners Ever 'Get It'?" http://rci.rutgers.edu/~redlawsk/papers/A%20Tipping%20Point%20Final%20Version.pdf.

9. Ibid.

10. Ibid.

11. James Kuklinski et al., "Misinformation and the Currency of Democratic Citizenship," *Journal of Politics* 62, no. 3 (August 2000): 790–816, https://www.unc.edu/~fbaum/teaching/articles/JOP-2000-Kuklinski.pdf.

12. Christopher Joyce, "Rising Sea Levels Made This Republican Mayor a Climate Change Believer," NPR.org, May 17, 2016, http://www.npr.org/2016/05/17/477014145/rising-seas-made-this-republican-mayor-a-climate-change-believer.

13. Ibid.

14. Erika Bolstad, "Florida Republicans Demand Climate Change Solutions," *Scientific American*, March 15, 2016, https://www.scientificamerican.com/article/florida-republicans-demand-climate-change-solutions/.

15. Brendan Nyhan and Jason Reifler, "The Roles of Information Deficits and Identity Threat in the Prevalence of Misperceptions," Feb. 24, 2017, https://www.dartmouth.edu/~nyhan/opening-political-mind.pdf.

16. Ruth Marcus, "Forget the Post-Truth Presidency: Welcome to the Pre-Truth Presidency," *Washington Post*, March 23, 2017, https://www.washingtonpost.com/opinions/welcome-to-the-pre-truth-presidency/2017/03/23/b35856ca-1007-11e7-9b0d-d27c98455440_story.html?utm_term=.86208421e389.

17. http://time.com/4710456/donald-trump-time-interview-truth-falsehood/.

18. Glenn Kessler and Michelle Ye Hee Lee, "President Trump's Cascade of False Claims in *Time*'s Interview on His Falsehoods," *Washington Post*, March 23, 2017, https://www.washingtonpost.com/news/fact-checker/wp/2017/03/23/president-trumps-cascade-of-false-claims-in-times-interview-on-his-falsehoods/?utm_term=.1df47d64641a; Michael Shear, "What Trump's *Time* Interview Shows about His Thinking," *New York Times*, March 23, 2017, https://www.nytimes.com/2017/03/23/us/politics/what-trumps-time-interview-shows-about-his-thinking.html?_r=0; Lauren Carroll and Louis Jacobson, "Fact-Checking Trump's TIME Interview on Truths and Falsehoods," *PolitiFact*, March 23, 2017, http://www.politifact.com/truth-o-meter/article/2017/mar/23/fact-checking-trumps-time-interview-truths-and-fal/.

19. Marcus, "Forget the Post-Truth Presidency."

20. http://time.com/4710456/donald-trump-time-interview-truth-falsehood/.

21. Lawrence Douglas, "Donald Trump's Dizzying *Time* Magazine Interview Was 'Trumpspeak' on Display," *Guardian*, March 24, 2017, https://www.theguardian.com/commentisfree/2017/mar/24/donald-trumps-dizzying-time-magazine-interview-trumpspeak.

22. Bill Moyers, "A Group of Experts Wrote a Book about Donald Trump's Mental Health—and the Controversy Has Just Begun," *Mother Jones*, Sept. 23, 2017, http://www.motherjones.com/politics/2017/09/a-group-of-experts-wrote-a-book-about-donald-trumps-mental-health-and-the-controversy-has-just-begun/.

23. https://science.ksc.nasa.gov/shuttle/missions/51-l/docs/rogers-commission/Appendix-F.txt.

BIBLIOGRAPHY

Abrams, Lindsay. "BBC Staff Ordered to Stop Giving Equal Airtime to Climate Deniers." *Salon*, July 6, 2014. http://www.salon.com/2014/07/06/bbc_staff _ordered_to_stop_giving_equal_air_time_to_climate_deniers/.

Arendt, Hannah. *The Origins of Totalitarianism*. New York: Harcourt, Brace, 1951.

Asch, Solomon. "Opinions and Social Pressure." *Scientific American* 193 (November 1955): 31–35.

Beck, Julie. "This Article Won't Change Your Mind." *Atlantic*, March 13, 2017.

Bedley, Scott. "I Taught My 5th-Graders How to Spot Fake News: Now They Won't Stop Fact-Checking Me." *Vox*, May 29, 2017. https://www.vox.com/first -person/2017/3/29/15042692/fake-news-education-election.

Benson, Ophelia, and Jeremy Stangroom. *Why Truth Matters*. London: Continuum, 2006.

Berube, Michael. "The Science Wars Redux." *Democracy Journal* (winter 2011): 64–74.

Blackburn, Simon. *Truth: A Guide*. Oxford: Oxford University Press, 2007.

Boghossian, Paul. *Fear of Knowledge*. Oxford: Oxford University Press, 2006.

Bolstad, Erika. "Florida Republicans Demand Climate Change Solutions." *Scientific American*, March 15, 2016. https://www.scientificamerican.com/article/ florida-republicans-demand-climate-change-solutions/.

Boykoff, Maxwell, and Jules Boykoff. "Balance as Bias: Global Warming and the US Prestige Press." *Global Environmental Change* 14 (2004): 125–136.

Braman, Donald, et al. "The Polarizing Impact of Science Literacy and Numeracy on Perceived Climate Change Risks." *Nature Climate Change* 2 (2012): 732–735.

Bridges, Tristan. "There's an Intriguing Reason So Many Americans Are Ignoring Facts Lately." *Business Insider*, Feb. 27, 2017.

Cadwalladr, Carole. "Daniel Dennett: 'I Begrudge Every Hour I have to Spend Worrying about Politics.'" *Guardian*, Feb. 12, 2017. https://www.theguardian .com/science/2017/feb/12/daniel-dennett-politics-bacteria-bach-back -dawkins-trump-interview.

Calcutt, Andrew. "The Truth about Post-Truth Politics." *Newsweek*, Nov. 21, 2016.

Coll, Steve. *Private Empire: ExxonMobil and American Power*. New York: Penguin, 2012.

Collin, Finn. *Science Studies as Naturalized Philosophy*. Synthese Library Book Series, vol. 348. New York: Springer, 2011.

Cunningham, Brent. "Rethinking Objectivity." *Columbia Journalism Review* 42, no. 2 (July–August 2003): 24–32. http://archives.cjr.org/united_states_pro ject/rethinking_objectivity_a_wisco.php.

DeSteno, David, and Piercarlo Valdesolo. "Manipulations of Emotional Context Shape Moral Judgment." *Psychological Science* 17, no. 6 (2006): 476–477.

Douglas, Lawrence. "Donald Trump's Dizzying Time Magazine Interview Was 'Trumpspeak' on Display." *Guardian*, March 24, 2017. https://www.theguard ian.com/commentisfree/2017/mar/24/donald-trumps-dizzying-time -magazine-interview-trumpspeak.

Edkins, Brett. "Donald Trump's Election Delivers Massive Ratings for Cable News." *Forbes*, Dec. 1, 2016.

Eilperin, Juliet. "Climate Skeptics Seek to Roll Back State Laws on Renewable Energy." *Washington Post*, Nov. 25, 2012.

Ellis, Justin. "Why the Huffington Post Doesn't Equivocate on Issues like Global Warming." *NiemanLab*, April 16, 2012. http://www.niemanlab.org/ 2012/04/why-the-huffington-post-doesnt-equivocate-on-issues-like-global -warming/

Farhl, Paul. "One Billion Dollars Profit? Yes, the Campaign Has Been a Gusher for CNN." *Washington Post*, Oct. 27, 2016.

Fessler, Daniel, et al. "Political Orientation Predicts Credulity Regarding Puta- tive Hazards." *Psychological Science* 28, no. 5 (2017): 651–660.

Fleeson, Lucinda. "Bureau of Missing Bureaus." American Journalism Review (October–November 2003). http://ajrarchive.org/article.asp?id=3409.

Frankfurt, Harry. *On Bullshit*. Princeton: Princeton University Press, 2009.

Frankfurt, Harry. *On Truth*. New York: Knopf, 2006.

Gabler, Neal. "Donald Trump Triggers a Media Civil War." *billmoyers.com* (blog), March 25, 2016. http://billmoyers.com/story/donald-trump-triggers-a-media -civil-war/.

Gandour, Ricardo. "Study: Decline of Traditional Media Feeds Polarization." *Columbia Journalism Review*, Sept. 19, 2016. https://www.cjr.org/analysis/ media_polarization_journalism.php.

Gibbs, Nancy. "When a President Can't Be Taken at His Word." *Time*, April 3, 2017.

Giere, Ronald. *Understanding Scientific Reasoning*. New York: Harcourt, 1991.

Gottfried, Jeffrey and Elisa Shearer, "News Use Across Social Media Platforms 2016." *Pew Research Center*, May 26, 2016.

Graves, Lucas. *Deciding What's True: The Rise of Political Fact-Checking in American Journalism*. New York: Columbia University Press, 2016.

Gross, Paul, and Norman Levitt. *Higher Superstition: The Academic Left and Its Quarrels with Science*. Baltimore: Johns Hopkins University Press, 1994.

Gross, P., N. Levitt, and M. W. Lewis, eds. *The Flight from Science and Reason*. New York: New York Academy of Sciences, 1996.

Gunther, Marc. "The Transformation of Network News." *Nieman Reports*, June 15, 1999. http://niemanreports.org/articles/the-transformation-of-network -news/.

Halberstam, David. *The Powers That Be*. Urbana: University of Illinois Press, 2000.

Hansen, James. "The Threat to the Planet." *New York Review of Books*, July 13, 2006. http://www.nybooks.com/articles/2006/07/13/the-threat-to-the -planet/.

Hansen, James. *Storms of My Grandchildren*. New York: Bloomsbury, 2009.

Healy, Melissa. "Why Conservatives Are More Likely Than Liberals to Believe False Information about Threats." *Los Angeles Times*, Feb. 2, 2017.

Higgins, Andrew, Mike McIntire, and Gabriel J. X. Dance. "Inside a Fake News Sausage Factory: 'This Is All about Income." *New York Times*, Nov. 25, 2016.

Hoggan, James, and Richard Littlemore. *Climate Cover-Up: The Crusade to Deny Global Warming*. Vancouver: Greystone, 2009.

Jones, Andrew. "Want to Better Understand 'Post-Truth' Politics? Then Study Postmodernism." *Huffington Post*, Nov. 11, 2016. http://www.huffingtonpost. co.uk/andrew-jones/want-to-better-understand_b_13079632.html.

Joyce, Christopher. "Rising Sea Levels Made This Republican Mayor a Climate Change Believer." *NPR*, May 17, 2016. http://www.npr.org/2016/05/17/ 477014145/rising-seas-made-this-republican-mayor-a-climate-change -believer.

Kahan, Dan M. "Climate-Science Communication and the Measurement Problem." *Advances in Political Psychology* 36 (2015): 1–43.

Kahan, Dan M., et al. "Cultural Cognition of Scientific Consensus." *Journal of Risk Research* 14 (2011): 147–174.

Kahneman, Daniel. *Thinking Fast and Slow*. New York: Farrar, Straus & Giroux, 2011.

Kanai, Ryota, Tom Feilden, Colin Firth, and Geraint Rees. "Political Orientations Are Correlated with Brain Structure in Young Adults." *Current Biology* 21, no. 8 (April 26, 2011): 677–680.

Kessler, Glenn, and Ye Hee Lee Michelle. "President Trump's Cascade of False Claims in Time's Interview on His Falsehoods." *Washington Post*, March 23, 2017.

Keyes, Ralph. *The Post-Truth Era: Dishonesty and Deception in Contemporary Life*. New York: St. Martin's, 2004.

Khazan, Olga. "Why Fake News Targeted Trump Supporters." *Atlantic*, Feb. 2, 2017.

Koertge, N., ed. *A House Built on Sand: Exposing Postmodernist Myths About Science*. Oxford: Oxford University Press, 2000.

Koppel, Ted. "Olbermann, O'Reilly and the Death of Real News." *Washington Post*, Nov. 14, 2010.

Kruger, Justin, and David Dunning. "Unskilled and Unaware of It: How Difficulties in Recognizing One's Own Incompetence Lead to Inflated Self-Assessments." *Journal of Personality and Social Psychology* 77, no. 6 (1999): 1121–1134.

Kuklinski, James, Paul J. Quirk, Jennifer Jerit, David Schwieder, and Robert F. Rich. "Misinformation and the Currency of Democratic Citizenship." *Journal of Politics* 62, no. 3 (Aug. 2000): 790–816.

Kurtzleben, Danielle. "With 'Fake News,' Trump Moves from Alternative Facts to Alternative Language." *NPR*, Feb. 17, 2017. http://www.npr.org/2017/02/17/515630467/with-fake-news-trump-moves-from-alternative-facts-to-alternative-language.

Latour, Bruno. "Why Has Critique Run out of Steam? From Matters of Fact to Matters of Concern." *Critical Inquiry* 30 (winter 2004): 225–248.

Lawrence, Jeff. "Communique Interview: Phillip E. Johnson." *Communique: A Quarterly Journal* (spring 1999).

Levitin, Daniel J. *Weaponized Lies: How to Think Critically in the Post-Truth Era*. New York: Dutton, 2016.

Longino, Helen. *Science as Social Knowledge: Values and Objectivity in Scientific Inquiry*. Princeton, NJ: Princeton University Press, 1990.

Lynch, Conor. "Trump's War on Environment and Science Are Rooted in His Post-Truth Politics—and Maybe in Postmodern Philosophy." *Salon*, April 1, 2017. http://www.salon.com/2017/04/01/trumps-war-on-environment-and-science-are-rooted-in-his-post-truth-politics-and-maybe-in-postmodern-philosophy/.

Lynch, Michael. *In Praise of Reason*. Cambridge, MA: MIT Press, 2012.

Lynch, Michael. *True to Life: Why Truth Matters*. Cambridge, MA: MIT Press, 2004.

Macur, Juliet. "Why Do Fans Excuse the Patriots' Cheating Past?" *New York Times*, Feb. 5, 2017.

Maheshwari, Sapna. "How Fake News Goes Viral: A Case Study." *New York Times*, Nov. 20, 2016.

Manjoo, Farhad. *True Enough: Learning to Live in a Post-Fact Society*. Hoboken, NJ: Wiley, 2008.

Marantz, Andrew. "Trolls for Trump: Meet Mike Cernovich, the Meme Mastermind of the Alt-Right." *New Yorker*, Oct. 31, 2016.

Marche, Stephen. "The Left Has a Post-Truth Problem Too: It's Called Comedy." *Los Angeles Times*, Jan. 6, 2017.

Marcus, Ruth. "Forget the Post-Truth Presidency: Welcome to the Pre-Truth Presidency." *Washington Post*, March 23, 2017.

Marusak, Joe. "Fake News Author Is Fired; Apologizes to Those Who Are 'Disappointed' by His Actions." *Charlotte Observer*, Jan. 19, 2017.

McIntyre, Lee. "The Attack on Truth." *Chronicle of Higher Education*, June 8, 2015.

McIntyre, Lee. *Dark Ages: The Case for a Science of Human Behavior*. Cambridge, MA: MIT Press, 2006.

McIntyre, Lee. *Respecting Truth: Willful Ignorance in the Internet Age*. New York: Routledge, 2015.

Mercier, Hugo, and Daniel Sperber. "Why Do Humans Reason? Arguments for an Argumentative Theory." *Behavioral and Brain Sciences* 34, no. 2 (2011): 57–111.

Meyer, Robinson. "The Rise of Progressive 'Fake News.'" *Atlantic*, Feb. 3, 2017.

Mooney, Chris. "Once and For All: Climate Denial Is Not Postmodern." *DeSmog Blog.com*, Feb. 28, 2011. https://www.desmogblog.com/once-and-all-climate -denial-not-postmodern.

Mooney, Chris. *The Republican Brain: The Science of Why They Deny Science— And Reality*. Hoboken, NJ: Wiley, 2012.

Mooney, Chris. *The Republican War on Science*. New York: Basic Books, 2005.

Nichols, Tom. *The Death of Expertise: The Campaign against Established Knowledge and Why It Matters*. Oxford: Oxford University Press, 2017.

Nyhan, Brendan and Jason Reifler. "The Roles of Information Deficits and Identity Threat in the Prevalence of Misperceptions." February 24, 2017. https://www.dartmouth.edu/~nyhan/opening-political-mind.pdf.

Nyhan, Brendan, and Jason Reifler. "When Corrections Fail: The Persistence of Political Misperceptions." *Political Behavior* 32, no. (2) (June 2010): 303–330.

Ohlheiser, Abby, and Ben Terris. "How Mike Cernovich's Influence Moved from the Internet Fringes to the White House." *Washington Post*, April 7, 2017.

Oreskes, Naomi, and Erik Conway. *Merchants of Doubts: How a Handful of Scientists Obscured the Truth on Issues from Tobacco Smoke to Global Warming.* New York: Bloomsbury, 2010.

Pennock, Robert. "The Postmodern Sin of Intelligent Design Creationism." *Science and Education* 19 (2010): 757–778.

Perez-Pena, Richard. "Newspaper Circulation Continues to Decline Rapidly." *New York Times*, Oct. 27, 2008.

Pew Research Center. "State of the News Media 2016: Newspapers Fact Sheet" (June 15, 2016). http://assets.pewresearch.org/wp-content/uploads/sites/13/2016/06/30143308/state-of-the-news-media-report-2016-final.pdf.

Pierson, David. "Facebook Bans Fake News from Its Advertising Network—but not Its News Feed." *Los Angeles Times*, Nov. 15, 2016.

Quine, W. V. O., and J. S. Ullian. *The Web of Belief*. New York: McGraw Hill, 1978.

Rabin-Havt, Ari. *Lies, Incorporated: The World of Post-Truth Politics*. New York: Anchor Books, 2016.

Redlawsk, David, et al. "The Affective Tipping Point: Do Motivated Reasoners Ever 'Get It'?" *Political Psychology* 31, no. 4 (2010): 563–593.

Resnick, Gideon. "Trump's Son Says Mike 'Pizzagate' Cernovich Deserves a Pulitzer." *The Daily Beast*, April 4, 2017. http://www.thedailybeast.com/trumps-son-says-mike-pizzagate-cernovich-deserves-a-pulitzer.

Samuel, Alexandra. "To Fix Fake News, Look to Yellow Journalism." *JStor Daily*, Nov. 29, 2016. https://daily.jstor.org/to-fix-fake-news-look-to-yellow-journalism/.

Schudson, Michael. *Discovering the News: A Social History of American Newspapers*. New York: Basic Books, 1973.

Seelye, Katharine. "Newspaper Circulation Falls Sharply." *New York Times*, Oct. 31, 2006.

Shane, Scott. "From Headline to Photograph, a Fake News Masterpiece." *New York Times*, Jan. 18, 2017.

Shear, Michael. "What Trump's Time Interview Shows about His Thinking." *New York Times*, March 23, 2017.

Shermer, Michael. *The Believing Brain*. New York: Times Books, 2011.

Silberman, G. 1993. "Phil Johnson's Little Hobby." *Boalt Hall Cross-Examiner* 6, no. 2 (1993): 1, 4, 9–10.

Snyder, Timothy. *On Tyranny: Twenty Lessons from the 20th Century*. New York: Tim Duggan Books, 2017.

Sokal, Alan. "A Physicist Experiments with Cultural Studies." *Lingua Franca* (May–June 1996).

Sokal, Alan. "Transgressing the Boundaries: Toward a Transformative Hermeneutics of Quantum Gravity." *Social Text* 46–47 (spring–summer 1996): 217–252.

Soll, Jacob. "The Long and Brutal History of Fake News." *Politico*, Dec. 18, 2016. http://www.politico.com/magazine/story/2016/12/fake-news-history-long-violent-214535.

Specter, Michael. *Denialism: How Irrational Thinking Hinders Scientific Progress, Harms the Planet, and Threatens Our Lives*. New York: Penguin, 2009.

Stanley, Jason. *How Propaganda Works*. Princeton, NJ: Princeton University Press, 2015.

Subramanian, Samantha. "Inside the Macedonian Fake-News Complex." *Wired*, Feb. 15, 2017.

Sunstein, Cass. *Infotopia: How Many Minds Produce Knowledge*. Oxford: Oxford University Press, 2006.

Tani, Maxwell. "Some of Trump's Top Supporters Are Praising a Conspiracy Theorist Who Fueled 'Pizzagate' for His Reporting." *Business Insider*, April 4, 2017.

Taylor, Adam. "Trump Loves a Conspiracy Theory: Now His Allies in the Fringe Media Want Him to Fall for One in Syria." *Washington Post*, April 7, 2017.

Thaler, Richard. *Misbehaving: The Making of Behavioral Economics*. New York: Norton, 2015.

Trivers, Robert. *The Folly of Fools: The Logic of Deceit and Self-Deception in Human Life*. New York: Basic Books, 2011.

Trump, Donald, with Tony Schwartz. *The Art of the Deal*. New York: Random House, 1992.

Viner, Katharine. "How Technology Disrupted the Truth." *Guardian*, July 12, 2016. https://www.theguardian.com/media/2016/jul/12/how-technology-disrupted-the-truth.

Warner, Judith. "Fact-Free Science." *New York Times Magazine*, Feb. 25, 2011.

Wason, P. C. "On the Failure to Eliminate Hypotheses in a Conceptual Task." *Quarterly Journal of Experimental Psychology* 12 (1960): 129–140.

Westen, Drew, et al. "Neural Bases of Motivated Reasoning: An fMRI Study of Emotional Constraints on Partisan Political Judgment in the 2004 U.S. Presidential Election." *Journal of Cognitive Neuroscience* 18, no. 11 (Nov. 2006): 1947–1958.

Wingfield, Nick, Mike Isaac, and Katie Benner. "Google and Facebook Take Aim at Fake News Sites." *New York Times*, Nov. 14, 2016.

Woolf, Christopher. "Back in the 1890s, Fake News Helped Start a War." *Public Radio International*, Dec. 8, 2016. https://www.pri.org/stories/2016-12-08/long-and-tawdry-history-yellow-journalism-america.

FURTHER READINGS

Blackburn, Simon. *Truth: A Guide*. Oxford: Oxford University Press, 2007.

Frankfurt, Harry. *On Bullshit*. Princeton, NJ: Princeton University Press, 2009.

Kahneman, Daniel. *Thinking Fast and Slow*. New York: Farrar, Straus & Giroux, 2011.

Lynch, Michael. *In Praise of Reason*. Cambridge, MA: MIT Press, 2012.

McIntyre, Lee. *Respecting Truth: Willful Ignorance in the Internet Age*. New York: Routledge, 2015.

Nyhan, Brendan, and Jason Reifler. "When Corrections Fail: The Persistence of Political Misperceptions." *Political Behavior* 32, no. 2 (June 2010): 303–330.

Oreskes, Naomi, and Erik Conway. *Merchants of Doubts: How a Handful of Scientists Obscured the Truth on Issues from Tobacco Smoke to Global Warming*. New York: Bloomsbury, 2010.

Rabin-Havt, Ari. *Lies, Incorporated: The World of Post-Truth Politics*. New York: Anchor Books, 2016.

Redlawsk, David, et al. "The Affective Tipping Point: Do Motivated Reasoners Ever 'Get It'?" *Political Psychology* 31, no. 4 (2010): 563–593.

Snyder, Timothy. *On Tyranny: Twenty Lessons from the 20th Century*. New York: Tim Duggan Books, 2017.

Stanley, Jason. *How Propaganda Works*. Princeton, NJ: Princeton University Press, 2015.

Trivers, Robert. *The Folly of Fools: The Logic of Deceit and Self-Deception in Human Life*. New York: Basic Books, 2011.

INDEX